BORN TO LIVE ON THE EDGE

"EXPERIENCES FROM LIVING ON A FARM TO FLYING COMBAT SORTIES IN VIETNAM TO RETIREMENT"

FREDRICK PUMROY

Published in the United States of America

ISBN 978-1-959173-27-4 (SC)
ISBN 978-1-959173-28-1 (HC)
ISBN 978-1-959173-26-7 (Ebook)

Pumroy Publishing
222 West 6th Street
Suite 400, San Pedro, CA, 90731
www.stellarliterary.com

Order Information and Rights Permission:

Quantity sales. Special discounts might be available on quantity purchases by corporations, associations, and others. For details, contact the publisher at the address above.

For Book Rights Adaptation and other Rights Permission. Call us at toll-free 1-888-945-8513 or send us an email at admin@stellarliterary.com.

ACKNOWLEDGMENTS

This book is dedicated to my parents; Bernard Neal Pumroy and Vera Lydia (Dahl) Pumroy, my wife; Mary Anne, my children; Leanna, Julia and Richard and eight grandchildren; Lauren, Daniel, Lacey, Rachael, Brooklyn, Jordan, Jackson and Madison.

My parents taught me the fundamentals of life to include Christian values, work ethic, and how to treat people. Mary was my mainstay. She was always there when I needed someone and practically raised the children by herself while I was off gaining exciting experiences. My children gave a sense of value and challenge as we tried to teach them the fundamentals and values of life Mary and I were taught. Evidently we did a good job as they are leading successful lives and continue the chain of teaching their children these same fundamentals and values of life.

Finally, I owe the path of life I took to almighty God who guided me throughout my life and saved me from death on several occasions.

BORN TO LIVE
ON THE EDGE

"With the help of God and all those who have influenced me, I was able to grow from my roots as a poor country boy from Indiana into a person with the desire to help people and promote American ideologies even though it involved doing things on the edge of failure or even death!"

FREDRICK PUMROY

FORWARD

This book is an account of the experiences of Fredrick L. Pumroy from birth to his retirement. It is based on real life experiences and how they impacted the life of those associated with him. It was mainly written to provide a historical document for his descendants, so they will know the trials and tribulations their father and grandfather went through.

Fred's reason for writing this book was to give an example of how a person growing up under poor economic conditions could be successful in life, and it also tries to answer the following question: Why do people do dangerous things even though it may cost them their lives? He also wanted to provide his extended family and all the other people living in these same kind of conditions the incentive to trust in God and follow the philosophy that "You can do whatever you put your mind to, if it is God's Will".

Table of Contents

CHAPTER ONE
Putting your Life on the Line

Ever wonder *why* there are "Soldiers of Fortune" or volunteers for special missions who put their life on the line to complete a mission? The Forward Air Controller (FAC) was one such breed of pilot. These pilots had balls of brass and were in the middle of every battle in the Viet Nam war.

Although the FACs had numerous special assignments, their main mission was to find enemy targets and destroy those targets by identifying them for the fighters and bombers assigned to them by the Airborne Command and Control Center (ABCCC). To mark these targets the FAC would fire a white phosphorous rocket in the vicinity of the target leaving a puff of white smoke, instruct the strike aircraft where the target was positioned relative to the FAC's smoke and would then clear the strike aircraft in "hot" on each pass. The term "Hit My Smoke" was used when the FAC's rocket would hit the target.

Once the lead strike aircraft had dropped its munitions the FAC would clear the next aircraft in "hot" to strike the target until either the aircraft were out of munitions or the target was destroyed. After the strike aircraft had gone back to home station the FAC stayed in the area to do a bomb damage assessment (BDA). This doesn't sound like it is too difficult until you realize that while doing these maneuvers the FAC was being fired upon by 50 Caliber, 23MM, 37MM or 57MM guns (or all of the above!!) while over the target. You could tell the pilots who had the "Right Stuff"; they were the ones who volunteered to take the most dangerous missions and were successful in completing their mission at whatever the cost.

Figure 1: This picture shows Captain Fred Pumroy next to an OV-10 aircraft getting ready for a mission at Nakon Phanom Air Base, Thailand in 1970

I had been lucky enough to avoid being hit once during a combat mission until after flying over the Ho Chi Minh Trail in Laos for about one month. Then I experienced the most dangerous situation of the tour. I was flying a mission over a portion of Laos on the borders of South Viet Nam and North Viet Nam called "Four Alpha" which was the most densely defended area we flew over. Four Alpha was where North Vietnam, South Vietnam and Laos borders joined. I had just arrived over the target and had a flight of four F-4s check in for the strike. I had located the target. It was a stock pile of supplies, approximately two or three semi loads worth hidden just off the road under tree cover. I had made my first rocket pass leaving a "White Phosphorus" mark just next to the target. As usual the 23MM and 37MM gunners started shooting as I rolled in. As I focused on the target I could see the tracers as they flashed past the cockpit. This is when your gut starts wrenching and it is all you can do to keep focus on the target and fighters.

I cleared the lead aircraft in "Hot". He rolled in and dropped his bombs. I rolled inverted to see where his bombs hit. They were just short of the target so I directed the second fighter to hit about 20 meters past his smoke. I rolled in parallel with the second fighter until he dropped his bombs, then just as I went inverted to see where he hit in relation to the target; I heard a loud explosion and the aircraft shook. I was hit by a 37 MM shell. This put me into a moment of terror as I knew if I went down in that area I would be killed or skinned alive, as they tortured the crewmen for information..

"I have been hit" I yelled over the radio. I rolled back straight and level to see what the damage was and try to regain my composure. The burst left a large hole in the side of the engine and froze the engine propeller in an unfeathered position. An unfeathered prop was like having speed brakes out – it killed a lot of lift though not enough to keep from flying.

The F-4 fighter lead asked me if I needed help and he would fly over and check me out. I called ABCCC "Hillsboro" to launch a rescue team as I thought there was something wrong with the aircraft. I couldn't maintain altitude. I looked down at the target and saw that the second fighter hit the target and some secondary explosions were going off. I told the rest of the flight "While lead checks me out you are all cleared in "Hot" just hit the smoke, we will be West of target".

The F-4 lead fighter came up on my wing and confirmed the hole in the engine but to my surprise also observed; "Nail 21 your center wing tank is still attached". One of the first things I did was jettison the rocket pods and center wing tank. What I didn't know was the maintenance people at Nakon Phanom (NKP), my home station, decided to safety wire our center wing tanks so we couldn't jettison them as we had been jettisoning too many of them after getting hit. I headed toward NKP, but had to keep jinking to keep from getting hit again. Well… I discovered that an OV-10 does not fly very well with a full center wing tank and an unfeathered propeller!!

I had been hit at about 5000 ft indicated and was loosing about 150 ft per minute. The mountains around me were about 6000 ft high so the only escape route left was to fly over the Ho Chi Minh trail and pray. Luckily I had just gotten to the area a few minutes prior and hadn't turned the center wing pump off yet, which meant the fuel was being pumped overboard after the main tank was full. However, even with this slow venting of fuel I couldn't keep level flight until I had descended to less than 1000 feet Above Ground Level (AGL)…needless to say this was not conducive to my longevity as I had the attention of every Zip Gunner on the Trail. The NVA Gunners missed a great opportunity, but then again you can't hit what you can't see (there were A LOT of trees between them and me!!). As my altitude got lower I had to fly with wings level to reduce my descent rate. I had about 50 miles to fly until getting into friendly territory. All I could do was pray and keep my wings level. It seemed like an eternity until the A One E Sandy's arrived to escort me back to NKP. They were a sight to behold. This is when I realized that I was one of those pilots who craved doing something dangerous and even thrived on it; even though I realized that it might cost me my life.

Fred returning to Nakon Phanom AB, Thailand on one engine after taking a hit by a 37MM shell in 1970

CHAPTER TWO
Living on the Edge Growing Up

As you grow up and go through life's variety of experiences, your attitudes and principles are based on these experiences. Growing up on the farm provided a good background for formulating my actions over the rest of my life. It made me realize the value of life and that there is a higher being controlling our environment. These experiences combined to make me the person I grew to be.

Though I can't remember anything until around 3 years old, it appears I had a mind of my own from the start. At the age of 3, I rode my stick horse down the road to see my grandfather who was working in the field. I knew he would give me a ride on the tractor, which always gave me a thrill! This was about a mile away from home and when my mother missed me she got overly upset, after all I was just going to see my Grandpa Joe who was working in the field in the back of the farm! He brought me home and came to my aid just in time to save a good licking.

When I was 5 years old, I received a two wheel bicycle for Christmas and rode it off the one foot high cement ramp in back of the barn. I guess I thought I was Evil Canevil. Of course the landing was a little off so the bike and I both crashed to the ground leaving a permanent two inch scar on my left hand and a bruised ego. The bloody hand wasn't near as heart breaking as the bent fender on the front wheel of my bike but I ended up with about eight stitches on the palm of my hand – one of my first battle wounds.

At the age of 8, my father purchased an old Army L4 aircraft trainer (Super Cub) which was fully aerobatic. He would let me fly it in the air and do loops, rolls, split Ss, anything but land and takeoff. Mother made him sell it the next year as she thought we might kill ourselves. Besides it was too costly to re-skin and paint the aircraft as required from the annual inspection. This triggered a deep desire in me to have my own airplane someday so I could experience the exhilaration and excitement I experienced that year.

At age 9, I would drive the "H" model – Farmall tractor in the field and through the woods. I was pretty successful except for one day driving through the woods I ran over a stump (eight to twelve inches high) and almost turned the tractor over as it went up on one wheel and back down. I slowed down after that – after all I couldn't reach the pedals sitting down so I had to drive standing up and use the leverage of the steering wheel to engage the clutch or brakes.

At age 10, my brother was chasing me in the cow barn for squirting him with cow's milk as he walked past me while I was washing the cow's utter and tits. As he was chasing me I slipped and fell face first in the gutter which was full of runny cow excretions. That was punishment enough so he left me alone while I ran to the milk house to take a quick shower. If he wasn't six years older than me I would have gotten back at him. This experience later helped me get through a unique experience I had while flying over Laos as a FAC.

At age 11, I graduated to the "M" model – Farmall tractor. I worked the fields with a disc and harrow. Dad wouldn't let me do plowing or planting until I was 12. Started playing basketball for the 6th grade team and played some little league baseball but couldn't make most of the practices or games as we had to milk 60 head of Holstein cows morning and night in addition to working in the fields.

At age 12, my dad bought my brother Russell and I a set of boxing gloves to teach us how to defend ourselves. Dad had dropped out of school and went to work for the railroad when he was 15 and by the time he was 16 he was sparing with the professional boxers out of Chicago using the thin boxing gloves of the time. So he knew how to box and showed us the technique of the jab. Well during our boxing instructions while my brother and I were sparing, I got carried away and jabbed with both hands a couple of times and landed a lucky punch to Russell's nose which started to bleed. He was so mad he said he was going to kill me. He was eighteen and I was a little guy but could out run him most of the time which was lucky for me. That would be our last lesson, as mother made father get rid of the gloves. Besides I didn't want to try it again as I would get pulverized.

At age 13, I found out just how strong my dad's punch was. My cousin Larry Joe had bought a pack of cigarettes and we were trying them out in back of the barn one weekend. We hid the pack in the grain room where we ground the corn and oats together to make feed for the cows. Dad found the pack of cigarettes and asked me if we were smoking. I said no. He asked me again and told us he had found the pack of cigarettes in the feed room. Again I denied it. He got in my face and said he would ask me one more time and if I knew what was good for me I would not lie as he couldn't stand to be lied to. I lied for the third time and he hit me with a jab in the stomach that threw me about 4-5 feet in the air against the cement wall of the barn. Needless to say, I didn't lie to him again.

At age 14, entered ninth grade and was doing the full range of work on the farm: milking, plowing, planting, irrigating, baling hay and harvesting crops. Sports were now starting to fill my spare time. Even though I was still only five feet tall and weighed 105 pounds, I was strong and agile so was being groomed to play basketball, baseball and track.

At age 15, as a sophomore I grew to five feet six inches tall and started on the junior varsity basketball team and ran track and cross country. Only filled in on the baseball team when they needed someone as I had too many daily chores to go to practice and play in the games. In basketball and track I could practice on my own. During the summer months I would shoot baskets in between picking up and unloading wagons of baled hay. For running practice I would run to the back of the farm to get the cows out of the pasture and herd them to the barn every morning and night.

One day while irrigating the corn fields, I was moving irrigation pipes that were 6 inches in diameter and 10 feet long from one location to the other in the corn field and during lunch an uncle from the city came out to take me in to eat. I jumped on his fender so I wouldn't get his new Buick dirty and he drove down the lane about 30 miles per hour, when he came up on a mud puddle. What he didn't know was the mud puddle was about a foot deep and about 20 feet long. When he felt the car dip he put on the brakes and I flew off the front. I held onto the emblem on the hood of the car which turned me toward the middle of the car. As I fell, the car front bumper hit me in the back and drove me into the mud dragging me the length of the mud puddle. Luckily I passed out when I hit the ground and wasn't hurt too badly, just a few scrapes and bruises. Went to the hospital to make sure there weren't any broken bones and had the cuts cleaned up. That was enough irrigation for that day and I walked in for lunch from then on. In the fall, I bought a small motor cycle to get to school to practice and play sports. Loved the speed and jumping moguls in the road. Didn't have an incident until one day I was riding with a passenger on the back and tried to jump a 10 foot long and 3 foot deep dip in the back lane – didn't quite make it and wiped out the cycle. Though I only had a few bruises, I had a hurt pride and the bikes front wheel was bent. I must have under estimated the weigh of the rider as the next day I flew over the same bump with a foot to spare.

At the age of 16, as a junior, I grew to 5 foot 10 inches and played on the varsity basketball team. Track and Cross Country weren't my favorite sports but I did place in several meets in both sports. Purchased an old 1950 Nash Rambler to get to school and now was starting to occasionally go to town on the weekend in between chores. The right seat folded down into a bed, so I filed the latch down so all I had to do was hit the seat with my elbow and it would fall back into the bed position. I tried it out on a date with a girl called Debbie one night and it failed as she told me to take her right home as she was not that "kind of girl". That was the last time I tried that on the first date at least.

Most of this summer was spent playing basketball at the Cedar Lake out door courts where most of the college basketball players went for pickup games. By the end of the summer I had developed into one of the best shots in the county.

My senior year had its ups and downs but overall was very successful. I was now 6 foot tall and had gained some strength lifting bales of hay, running cross country and playing basketball. The fall started with Cross Country and I had won all the dual meets going in to the County Meet. In the County Meet, with about ¼ mile left in the 2 mile race, I stepped in a hole on the side of a hill and cracked a couple of bones in my left foot. I finished the race but one of my teammates beat me at the line and I came in second.

Our next meet was the Sectional and my foot still hadn't healed so I ran with a limp which caused me to get stomach cramps about half way through the race. I ended up in 11th place though and the other runners performed good enough for the team to get second place. We ended up being the only school with an enrollment of under 100 in High School to ever break into the top 10 in the State Cross Country Meet – we ended up tied for 8th. I ended up 66th which was about 40 or 50 people behind where I should have been if I had been able to run as I had when healthy.

Basketball started badly but ended up on a high note. I was still favoring a sore foot and couldn't shoot as accurately as I was supposed to and was trying too hard as I knew everyone was counting on me. As I went so did our team, we lost 3 of our first 5 games. Then Coach Grey let me play the entire game against Highland H.S. which was 5th in the state rankings – I made 25 points and averaged above 15 points a game thereafter. Emotionally I wasn't ready for all the pressure as I was a year younger than the other senior players but expected to perform as well.

The only team in the county we had problems with was Boone Grove, they beat us in the County Tourney but we beat them during the regular season to become co-champions of the county. By the end of the year our team began to jell and even Valparaiso (a school with over 1000 in H.S.) was afraid to play us. Well for our misfortune we drew them first in the Sectional and their two 6 foot 6 inch forwards, a 6 foot 2 inch center who could dunk back handed with both hands from a standing position, and two 6 foot guards were more than we could handle.

Spring continued to be successful as our Track team won most of our dual meets, the county conference championship and the County Track Meet. I took first place in the 440 yard race and the mile relay in the County Track Meet, but didn't make it out of the sectional meet.

That summer was one of not knowing where I was going; worked construction and received a few scholarship offers for Cross Country and Track (Valparaiso University, Eastern Michigan, Texas A&M and Ball State). My dad didn't have any extra money as he rented our farm and didn't make much income, so he couldn't afford any college expenses. Coach Grey convinced me to visit Ball State which is where he attended. I met Bob Lindsey, athletic director and some student athletes, some of who I had known from athletics in the county. I felt at home there, so I decided to go to Ball State on a grant and aid scholarship.

Leaving the farm was a big decision since that was all I had known – even though I didn't like it. Plus I didn't know if I could make it through college; my grades weren't very good, and I still hadn't read a book completely through up to that point due to the eye problem I continued to have. This is where I feel that sports activities, whether you are successful or not, help give individuals the confidence to try different things. Further, even though I knew that I might fail, it was worth the try just to get off the farm and experience something new.

CHAPTER THREE
College Days

My freshman year in college was a challenge. It was hard keeping up with studies, work and sports. Held my own in the academic area with passing grades and sports achievements were many.

I made the varsity cross country, basketball and track teams. Track was my best sport as I won the two mile race on a cinder track at a record pace – 10 minutes and 13.9 seconds. I was second fastest on the cross country team and a sub on the basketball team (sat the bench mostly though I could out run them all).

I supplemented the Grant and Aid Scholarship by working in the dorm cafeteria, cleaning tables and washing dishes. The only bad incident I had was when my roommate volunteered to rub down my legs after one of our track meets. He used some hot liquid rubbing compound and let some run down my butt crack onto my scrotum. I made the mistake of running into the shower to wash it off which soaked it further into the skin and it burned even more. I was so mad that when I went back into the room I cussed him out and started hitting him. The councilor broke the fight up and moved us into separate rooms immediately. We were never friends again, though I was probably wrong in hitting him, I had thought that he had done it on purpose.

During summer break, I made some extra money by applying liquid nitrogen to the corn crops around the area using my dad's tractor and an applicator I rented from a neighbor. My profit for this work was over $3500. Of course that didn't keep me out of trouble as I had to show my high school classmates, Fred Haman and Fred Simic, how tough I was.

Fred Simic had taken a boxing class at Indiana University and brought his boxing gloves with him. We met in downtown Kouts one evening and started to spar in the parking lot. He was jabbing me pretty good until I switched to a right handed jab and hit him with a left hook that put him flat on his back. We then went to a party we were invited to in Valparaiso. There were several people we knew there and we were having fun until one of the Valparaiso ex-wrestlers had a couple too many drinks and decided he wanted to start a fight with me. Finally after he said some disgusting statements about my mother, I invited him outside. He was a burly guy but a little shorter than I.

There was a bright yard light mounted on the house, so I would keep my back to the light and move my head so the light would shine in his eyes. Then I would jab him in the face a couple of times and set him up again. He finally got frustrated with this and tried to use his wrestling skills to get me down on the ground. Luckily I had only a couple of drinks and was faster than he was so he never did get me down. Then we heard the sirens, someone had called the police. My opponent told me they would meet us in the grave yard in an hour. We had heard of this happening before, where the guys from Valparaiso would go to the grave yard to fight, would have people hiding behind the tomb stones, and would gang up on their opponents. So we decided to make it a night and went home.

In the morning, I discovered I had a fat lip. Evidently, on one jab must have connected.

My sophomore year was a lot better. In Cross Country our team was undefeated in dual meets and was rated number one in the nation for Division II schools. Five times we had five of us finish first holding hands as we crossed the finish line, otherwise I would finish 2nd or 3rd on the team. The only let down we had was in the NCAA meet where we were predicted to win hands down. There were 130 runners lined up five deep, the course was on a golf course in Chicago, the temperature was in the low 20s and the first leg was one quarter of a mile to a 90 degree turn around a green on the golf course. I started third in line and was in the first 50 runners when I reached the green. As we turned the corner, someone stepped on my foot and their spikes tore through my shoe and pulled it off my foot. I tumbled to the ground and by the time I could get up I was behind about 100 runners. I worked my way up to the top fifty by the time we finished but I needed to beat 2 more runners for the team to come in first.

We came in second and coach Staley wouldn't talk to us all the way home and falling was no excuse. I felt so bad I went to a local bar with some of my fraternity brothers, who I had just pledged with that fall, and had a couple of beers to drown my sorrow. The bartender new I was 19 years old (you needed to be 21 in Indiana) but didn't say anything unless we got loud.

At around 1:00 in the morning some guy who was drunk came over and hit me on the side of the head and knocked me off my chair. I didn't even know him. I got up and rustled him to the floor and started hitting him with a barrage of punches. My fraternity brothers pulled me off him and told me to get in my car and drive home immediately as the bar maid had called the police. My old 1950 Plymouth wouldn't start right away and by the time I did get it started, as I drove out of the parking lot, the police drove in. I sped to my apartment which was in illegal housing above a drug store. The police recognized the car and knew where I lived. They busted into my apartment and took me to jail.

I thought, *Pumroy, what have you done now? You just might have ruined your live!* After the booking, I hitch hiked to the Campus Police station to talk to the officer who hired me as their janitor. I told him my story and he made a phone call to the Muncie police. He then told me to be in court on Monday, plead guilty and ask for mercy from the court.

The judge played along and scared me to death by reading a bunch of ordinances I had violated. He then fined me $25 and court costs for running a stop light. However, my real penalty was getting kicked off the basketball team.

I went home on vacation the next weekend and played basketball with some old school mates. One of them played on an industrial league team and they were looking for a point guard and asked me if I would play with them. I said yes if they would buy gas for me to help me get back home for the games. They filled my car with gas, gave me a meal and a six pack of beer. We won ever game except one – when we played the Prisoners in the Michigan City Prison - what an experience that was. One side of the court was betting on us and the other side for their team. When we were warming up the prisoners would come down to courtside and tell us if we knew what was good for us we would loose or win which ever way they were betting. These guys could have played professional basketball as they were in excellent shape, tough and good shots.

We lost this game but won the league tournament. I averaged over 20 points a game and had over 30 points during several games. Needless to say the coaches at Ball State weren't too happy with me. I was able to keep my scholarship in track and cross country though my performance was never as good the rest of my college career as I had picked up something in my bronchial tube (suspected frost bite) which caused me to cough up blood after I had run a mile or two. I didn't practice and would only run the meets. Our team still was winning most of our meets as the rest of the team was still doing very well.

During this year, I also discovered girls which hurt my study time and sports performances. I also put God on the back burner and concentrated on activities ... lets say a Christian would not be proud of.

One evening while entertaining a couple of ladies with my fraternity brother Roger, we heard a loud crash and looked out our upstairs window to discover that my car had disappeared. Well, Faith, a sister of Hope and Charity, was intoxicated while driving and hit my car as well as a couple of others. The police brought Faith to the house after they apprehended her as she wanted to offer a trade in lieu of us claiming the accident as she had had several accidents that year already. Since we were already tied up we declined and I went ahead and filed a claim to the insurance company. They paid me $75 which wasn't bad since I had paid my brother $50 for the car in the first place.

The problem that was this incident was brought to the attention of the Dean of Men, Mr. Collier, who happened to own the house next door and was also a Sig Tau (fraternity brother of ours). Our only option was to move back into the fraternity house as we were living in unauthorized housing.

The accident ruined my radiator and starter so I moved my car to the fraternity house and parked it in the back of the house. It was then used as a sleeping place for those of us who didn't get their date back to the dorm before curfew.

I was dating four different girls over a nine month period during my junior year; two lived in the same dorm, when I was introduced to Mary (who later became Mrs. Pumroy). She was not only beautiful; she was a real nice girl. I went out with her a few times (though I would still see some of my other friends on occasion) until one night I took her to Fort Wayne which was her home. I carried her across her back yard so she wouldn't have to walk through the mud. When I got to the door her mother opened the door and whispered something in her ear. She said good night and thanks for bringing her home but didn't invite me in to meet her parents. This infuriated me, so when I got to the nearest gas station I called her house and she informed me that her boy friend was at the house and she didn't want to let him know about me.

I didn't go out with her for the rest of the school year. Besides I didn't have time as I was still running, playing basketball, riding the bike for the annual bike-a-thon and seeing the other girls again.

Over the winter I ran into another girl named Fran and she was from South Bend. After one of our basketball games in South Bend I had the guys drop me off at her place. Her parents were gone and my parents had gone on a two day vacation, so I had to be home by 4:00 AM to milk the cows. Well her parents, who owned a Senior Home Center, had left her their brand new Chevy Impala to use. So we started driving to Kouts. The weather was icy so she had me drive. I was going about 55 miles an hour on Hwy 30 when I hit a rut in the road and the car started spinning, but before I could get it under control we were headed for a deep ditch, hit a telephone pole and rolled upside down back into the ditch.

It took a couple of hours before the police found her father and when he got there he wasn't too happy I had totaled his car. No more sex that night! The police took me to the next town which was Wanatah. It was about 1:30 in the morning and only one bar was open. However to my surprise three of my basketball teammates were still there. They gave me a ride home but I didn't think I would live through it. The guy was going between 60 and 70 miles per hour on pure icy back roads. When we drove out of Lacrosse, a small town about 5 miles from my home, the car started to spin. All I could see was another deep ditch we were headed for, but somehow he got the car straightened out and got me home safely. I was awfully lonely milking the cows that morning, so I was not sure all the excitement was worth it.

Fran's father gave me specific directions never to see her again. So I went back to school and dated my four previous friends.

During the winter, I also coached and played for the fraternity basketball team named the "Sig Tau Blues". We won most of our games and ended up as runner-up in the end of season tournament.

During the spring, in addition to running track, I also rode on the fraternity bike team which won the race for the second straight time that year. I also started to fly the Cessna 172 in the Flight Instruction Program (FIP) sponsored by AFROTC.

During summer break I hitchhiked to Eglin Air Force Base, Fort Walton Beach, Florida to attended AFROTC summer camp (it is a six week boot camp similar to what an Airman goes through when enlisting). I had to cut my hair off and eat square meals (eyes straight ahead, moving your arms and hands in a perpendicular motion getting the food and putting it in your mouth). I was the resident jock and won most of the competitive events to include being the pitcher on the fast pitch team.

During a rare, free few minutes one morning I wrote a letter to Mary. I knew she lived in Ft. Wayne, Indiana but didn't have her address, so I mailed it to Ft. Wayne without an address stating it was unknown. A good hearted mail person found a way to get it delivered.

When the camp was over I hitchhiked back to Ft. Wayne and crashed a friend's wedding reception in Fort Wayne as I knew Mary would be there – I don't think she was impressed with my butch haircut. Luckily, she didn't have a date that night, so I was able to be with her for a few hours. Mary and I started going together again in the fall of my senior year, so I terminated relationships with the other four girls I had been seeing.

Though I couldn't competitively run any more I went to all the Cross Country practices to help the coach with the new runners. I also continued to fly and obtained my private flying license. Of course I couldn't wait until I soloed so I could buzz the school during a football game. Luckily no one reported me.

In the winter, Mary and I decided to get married and set the date for 25 April 1964. Basketball was still a major part of my life as I remained coach of the fraternity team and played on my hometown industrial league team. Both teams won their respective leagues.

In the spring, I continued to train on the bike as this would be the third year in a row we would win the bike-a-thon a feat no one else had accomplished.

Four weeks before the race and two weeks before our wedding Roger Wisley and I were riding our usual 30 mile course and were racing into town at about 1:30 in the morning. He was on the outside of the road and I was on the inside. As we approach an intersection an on-coming car using no signals turned in front of us. I couldn't go to the outside and another car was coming at a high rate of speed on the inside. I decided to hit the turning car head on and leaped in the air just before I hit. *I thought, Pumroy your going to die this time!*

Just before I hit the car, I jumped just enough to clear the emblem on the old Buick but caught the left broken mirror as I skimmed the windshield and did a perfect dive over the left fender landing on my shoulder and rolling up to a standing position in a hedge around the adjacent house.

As I was cussing the drunken driver out for ruining my bike, Roger came over and said my pant leg was ripped and that I should take a look at it. When I lifted the pant leg up I discovered the cut was clear through to the bone. We went to the hospital, where it took over 50 stitches to sew my leg back together. I spent the next week in the hospital recuperating.

Next was the wedding reception, where Roger, Jake and Tom (all football players) plus my brother-in-law were in the wedding party. The three of them had football scrimmage that afternoon, so we left right afterward practice for Ft. Wayne to attend the rehearsal. As we approached Ft. Wayne we discovered the main bridge was out do to heavy rains so we had to deviate from our route and got lost. Well, one case of beer and three hours later we finally got to the rehearsal. It had been over for over an hour – Mary's parents weren't too happy by now though they did invite everyone to the rehearsal dinner. The guys told Mary's parents "not to worry as they had been in several weddings and knew what to do".

That night the boys took me out on the town for the bachelor party. Before the night was over I had lost my crutches and my leg was starting to swell down to my toes. We stayed over night at Roger's house and in the morning we crawled out of bed to get ready for the wedding which was across town and about a half hour drive. After a couple of fried eggs and bloody Mary's to get rid of our hangovers, we started dressing the groomsmen and myself. As they finished they got into their car and drove to the wedding. By the time Roger and I had finished dressing all the others had gone, which left us with no car.

With the wedding scheduled to start in about a half hour, we decided to call a cab. However Bruce came to the rescue and had remembered we

17

didn't have a car. (Bruce was the supplier of the beer since his father owned a beer distributing company).

We finally arrived at the church about 10 minutes late, I was in the back seat and as I slid out of the car dragging my bad leg, 3 or 4 beer cans fell out onto the parking lot. By now my mother-in-law was about to disown me. We were ushered to the side door of the Sanctuary and the wedding went smoothly except for when I had to kneel down. The old shoes I had to wear due to my swollen foot had "I" written on the left shoe and "do" written on the right shoe, just below the holes that were worn through. Even with all the snafus the wedding and reception went well. Mary and I went to Muncie that night to the apartment I had rented in the attic of a house near the campus for our honeymoon. We attended classes as normal the next couple of weeks.

On the Thursday before the Bike-a-thon race I went to the Sigma Tau Gama fraternity house for a meeting and the bike team was about ready to go out for a practice ride of over 20 miles. I couldn't resist and got on one of the bikes and rode around the block to see how my leg was feeling. It was a little sore but I decided to see how it would hold up for a 20 mile hike. After about 5 miles the leg got numb and didn't hurt at all. The only problem I had was getting off and exchanging the bike to another rider. During the team meeting when we returned I told Larry, the coach, that I would be able to ride but couldn't exchange. So we decided I could ride the first leg of the 50 mile race and when the field would catch up with me I would do the exchange on the inside lane so I could fall and roll to the side of the track after the other rider took control of the bike.

When Steve House, who had broken his ankle playing basketball about 3 weeks earlier, found out that I was going to ride, he decided he would ride also. So the night before the race we had a group photo taken with Steve and I on crutches. The significance of this was that our team had won the race the previous two years and this would be the third year in a row - a feat no one had done before. I rapped my 50 stitches with an ACE bandage and Steve cut his cast off with a power saw.

During the race, I held the lead for the first 10 miles and did my exchange without falling down and tearing more stitches. We won the race by over a quarter of a mile and became the heroes of the moment. This was one of those moments when it paid to have an understanding wife; Mary was a trouper and didn't complain.

The rest of the year was spend making sure I passed all the courses I was taking since I was not an "A" student as you could presume with all my extra curricular activities. Though it was close, I made it through and received my bachelor of science degree. Now I needed to concentrate on transitioning into the real world since Mary was pregnant and I was about to be commissioned into the Air Force. I pleaded my case to Capt Chase who was my mentor in the AFROTC program. He made some phone calls and got me into the first Pilot Training class (66-A) at Laughlin AFB, Del Rio, Texas scheduled for 10 July 1964.

After graduation, Mary and I moved in with my grandpa Joe Dahl and helped work the farm. We both woke up at around 4:30 A.M. each morning. I went to the barn to milk cows and Mary helped make breakfast for the workers (good experience for a city girl). I had bought a Volkswagen "bug" with all the money I had saved up and didn't have any loans to pay off so we were okay financially except for the trip to Del Rio, Texas. We had to make it to Laughlin AFB where I would start pilot training. We also had to wait one month after reporting in to get our first paycheck. Luckily grandpa Joe had given us $300 for helping him on the farm, which covered the first month's rent and some money for food. During this time, I began to realize how important it was for me to put my trust back into God's hands, as now I have a wife and child on the way. Mary helped during this transition, since she was a devout Christian and gave me a good example to follow.

CHAPTER FOUR
Pilot Training

Mary and I arrived in Del Rio on 9 July and when we passed Laughlin AFB we saw smoke coming from an airplane that had looked like it had crashed at the end of the runway. The local news that night reported that a student had crashed turning final and had been killed. This was not the best news for your new bride to hear just before starting pilot training.

I reported on 10 July and was immediately scheduled for a physical exam. I knew my eyes were bad and didn't need this exam to ruin my chances of becoming an Air Force pilot. There were six of us who failed the eye examination. Five were AFROTC graduates and one was an Academy grad. What I didn't know prior to getting there was the first two classes of each year were made up of 50% Academy graduates and 50% AFROTC distinguished graduates. For some reason, only known by the Almighty, only the Academy grad and I received a waiver, the other four students were "Washed Out" and sent to Navigator school.

The class started with 53 students in our "A" Flight (we were the first class at Del Rio to fly the supersonic T-38 aircraft). I studied hard and because I had flown some with my dad and the Flying Farmers I had a good feel for flying and was able to stay in the top seven for most of the T-37 phase of the class.

Mary was due to deliver our baby in August but was late, so the pressure kept building. At the end of August, I also had a final exam for an Aerodynamics course. This was the first time I was in jeopardy of getting washed out of training – I failed it on the first attempt. I was so

20

tense during the exam that I froze and had to take it verbally in order to pass.

On the 9th of September, Leanna Sue was born. This really changed our lives. Now there was another mouth to feed, but it also helped to take the pressure off, as she was a beautiful and healthy little girl. By now Mary knew the emergency procedures for each airplane better than I did, so while rocking Leanna to sleep she would have me recite the procedures until I had them down 100 percent correct.

Then, in early December, a few of us went to Mexico for a party and two of us picked up "infectious – Type B" Hepatitis. I had scheduled leave for two weeks over the Christmas holidays to show off our new baby girl (Leanna Sue). When we arrived at my parent's house in Kouts, Indiana I thought I had caught the flu and was carrying between 102 and 104 degree temperature. A doctor had given me penicillin shot but it didn't help.

T-37 aircraft used for initial training in 1964 at Laughlin AFB, Del Rio, Texas.

We spent New Years Eve with Mary's parents and went out with some friends to a party during which I tried to drink a Whiskey Sour and immediately threw it up.

We made it back to Del Rio, and my instructor came by to see how we were doing. He had his girlfriend with him who was a nurse and she told me to go directly to the doctor the next morning as I looked jaundice and one of the other students had contacted Hepatitis.

I spent the next two months in the hospital with the other student flat on our backs. I still had one T-37 ride plus three check rides to complete the first portion of the pilot training course. After another month on convalescent leave and being placed back two classes into "C" class, I was back under the pressure. They gave me one flight in each category (navigation, instrumentation and formation) to practice up.

However, during, the instrument mission, we had a one of a kind failure. I was under the hood (a visor that covered your peripheral view) flying a VOR approach. As we got to the fix at which point I would lower the gear for the descent, both engines quit and it went deathly silent in the airplane. I ran the checklist for in-flight engine failure, which was "Battery switch to emergency and starter switch to in-flight start". I tried two times and it didn't start. The "brand new" instructor yelled we have to eject – we are getting too low.

I said "I have a gut feel it will start this time – give me one more chance".

I hit the starter switch and the RPM for both engines started to "wind up" increase, but the instructor started to panic.

"We have to punch out now," he said. As he was just about to pull the ejection handles the airplane had started and was leveling off. We had made it.

Since I was still under the hood and hadn't looked outside, I didn't realize the terrain height there was about a thousand feet higher than at Laughlin AFB and there was no runway to land on. Therefore we were less than 100 feet above the ground when we came out of the descent. The rule of thumb was that if you ejected below 1500 feet the odds of making a successful ejection was 60 percent. Almighty God was looking after me again while I continued to Live on the Edge. Although I was starting to feel as if He might be trying to tell me that flying was not good for my health.

I did okay in the navigation and instrument flights but had a hard time with the formation flight. I would "grey" out under more than three "G" forces, so during a loop over maneuver and split "S" maneuver I couldn't see the other aircraft I was in trail with, I could only feel the edge of the jet wash (turbulent air from the engines). So I fell out of position twice which should have failed me but since the instructor new I was sick and had the ability, he only gave me a "fair" grade.

Now it was my turn at the T-38 super sonic Talon aircraft. I still experienced some slight grey out when doing transition (loops, Split "S", etc.) in the T-38 but was conscious enough to complete the maneuver satisfactorily. I kept getting stronger so the rest of the course in the T-38 was uneventful except for one solo flight at night when I did some rolls at

T-38 aircraft used for primary training in 1964 at Laughlin AFB, Del Rio, Texas.

night in the descent from 20 thousand feet to the over head pattern which was at 5000 feet. At the end of the last roll I had misread my altimeter by 10000 feet but looked out and saw aircraft above me, so I immediately put it in afterburner to climb. I don't know how low I got but I think it was below 500 feet. I reentered the pattern at 5000 feet and called in hoping no one saw me. It was a good experience check on landing with high adrenalin as I made a couple of touch and go landings before making a final full stop landing. *I thanked God for giving me the intuition to recover from a mistake before I joined the other pilots that were not so lucky. How many lives would I be given?*

Another exciting experience was when we took a trip to Las Vegas on an overnight cross country mission. We stayed out visiting the gambling tables until around 4:30 in the morning, although we had planned to takeoff on the return leg in the late afternoon. This wasn't too smart on my part since I still tired easily and couldn't drink more than one or two drinks.

At about 6:30 the base Squadron Commander called our lead Instructor to direct us to return to Del Rio immediately as there was a large storm with numerous tornados coming through the area crossing our flight path and they needed the airplanes back for the next days flights. Only one of our students hadn't drank the night before so we had several "hung over" pilots including the instructors. The sober student did the flight planning and the rest of us copied his plan. We made it to the airplane and immediately went on 100% oxygen which helped a little.

During taxi, I looked in the rear view mirror to discover my instructor had already fallen asleep. So I took off in formation with one of the other students and let him sleep. When we started the descent to the first landing base he woke up "startled" and asked where we were. I told him I didn't know I was just following the other pilot. He gave me a break the next leg to get a few minutes sleep so I could make it on to Laughlin AFB and finish my graded flight.

One morning (around 2:00 A.M.), Ben Yglasias, one of my class mates and a friend of his decided to climb up on our roof and yell some pretty vulgar statements (even for me) through the exhaust duct. They had been to Mexico and had a few too many drinks. Normally this wouldn't bother me but the next morning I had to get up at 4:30 A.M. to get ready for a Test Flight. They kept it up for over 30 minutes and I finally had enough and opened my pen flare container I had for emergencies only. I went outside and told Ben if he didn't get down I would shoot him with the flare gun. He still wouldn't get down. Earl my neighbor then came out with a 45 Caliber hand gun to see what was going on as he thought we were getting robbed or something. Maria, Earl's wife had called the police. Ben still wouldn't come down. I told him that if he didn't come down by the count of three I would fire the flare gun at him.

One...Two... Three – *bang*. I shot the flare in the vicinity of Ben. He let out a hoop as some of the sparks from the flare hit him in the shirt and burnt holes in it. He called me a crazy SOB but got down from the roof. You could hear the police car sirens by this time, so I told Ben and his friend to get moving unless they wanted to spend the night in jail. When the police got there I told them Ben had gone in the opposite direction. So he got home safely.

The next day, after my flight, I told the student flight commander about the incident so we told Ben the Wing commander wanted to see him over lunch hour about the incident (though he really didn't know anything about it). The Colonel usually went for a 5 mile run over his lunch hour. So I went in the Colonel's office with Ben and told him that I wouldn't jeopardize my career for his stupidity.

Just before the end of the lunch hour I told Ben I was leaving and he would have to face the Colonel alone. Just before the Colonel got back from his run the flight commander went in and told Ben it was just a joke.

Ben didn't think it was funny but I didn't think that what he had done the night before was funny either.

I did try one other maneuver that most student pilots tried during a solo flight which was to accelerate to supersonic flight and climb almost straight up until running out of airspeed to see if you could get over the 10 mile mark of 52, 800 feet. I went over 50 but couldn't quite make it to 52 thousand feet as my airspeed ran out and the aircraft was starting to stall. If the T-38 stalled and went into a flat spin you couldn't get it out so we were real careful of staying away from this condition.

I was one of the lucky ones, as we had 53 students when we started the course and 32 when we finished. Eight students were killed and the rest washed out for one reason or the other - killed, medical disqualification, air sickness, couldn't land, failed more than two classes or flights, etc.

I finished ranked seventh from the bottom of the class which ended up being a blessing as all the students who were ranked in the top ten of the class received F-105 aircraft assignments and all were killed or shot down and became a Prisoner of War (POWs).

I ended up in the KC-135 program which was better than the B-52 but everyone avoided it because of the Alert requirements (one week on alert and one week off with very little flying time).

CHAPTER FIVE
First Assignment to
Strategic Air Command (SAC)

Out of Pilot training, I was originally assigned to K.I. Sawyer AFB, Michigan and had orders to Fairchild AFB, Washington for Survival training on the way to Castle AFB, Merced, California for advanced pilot training. Three of us (Guess who? "Ben Yglasias, Ross Dewitt and myself") arrived at Fairchild. They said our orders had changed and we were to have reported at Castle AFB two days prior. So we went to a casino in Reno, Nevada to prepare for our trip to California. We arrived at Castle AFB the next morning after driving straight through. They told us we were supposed to have arrived at Castle AFB the week prior and they had replaced us with three other students. Personnel at Castle told us to report to our permanently assigned station.

I arrived at K.I. Sawyer AFB in November 1965 and was assigned several administrative duties to include director of training, scheduling assistant and staff officer for the squadron commander. I tried out for and made the Base basketball team and was the only officer on the team. We had a winning season but didn't perform too well in the Strategic Air Command tournament. I enjoyed it though and it gave me some success while waiting for my reassignment to Castle. The other advantage I had was I didn't have to pull alert as I could not be certified in the Emergency War Orders until I was checked out in the airplane but could fly with an instructor. I flew a couple of missions a week with the Standardization and Evaluation crews compiling over 20 hours a month. This gave me an edge when I finally attended the primary flight course at Castle in July 1966.

After getting checked out in the KC-135, I volunteered as third pilot in the B-52 Chrome Dome missions which flew over the North Pole on airborne alert requiring three refuelings and taking 24 hours flying time. I was able to log over 100 hours of flight time doing this though I didn't get much stick time. I knew most of the other co-pilots were getting out at the first opportunity to join the airlines as they had remained in the right seat for 5-6 years as a co-pilot before getting upgraded to first pilot. One reason for this was the lack of flying hours and it took 500 hours in the airplane before you could upgrade. So I volunteered for all the missions I could to build my hours up.

The best missions were flying out of Thailand on Young Tiger missions. They were 3-5 hours each and you flew every day on combat missions over the Gulf of Tonkin and Laos refueling fighters going into North Vietnam. The tours lasted 2-3 months and we would fly over 120 hours per month. Since I flew with instructor pilots most of the time I was able to fly the left seat (first pilot position). The missions were always exciting and varied.

On July 20, 1966, we had another addition to the family. Julia Lynn was born while I was on alert at K.I. Sawyer AFB. The timing couldn't have been worse as I was pitching in an inter-league softball game when I received word that Mary had delivered Julia. Mary was doing fine, so I finished pitching the ball game, which we lost by one run in the 11th inning. Mary, being a good military wife, handled the situation by herself, though my mother flew in to take care of Leanna while Mary was in the hospital. Of course my absence was highly noticed by my mother and in-laws.

In 1967, most of our missions out of Utapao, Thailand were over the Gulf of Tonkin. One particular sortie I remember was when a tanker in the cell in front of us was called to air refuel a Navy tanker who in turn off loaded fuel to a Navy fighter. All three were hooked up together and returned to a safe base in South Vietnam, a first in the air refueling business.

We landed five times with less than five thousand pounds of fuel left in our tanks (two of these missions were when we I was in the left seat). The significance of this was after the gauges read 3500 pounds of fuel you were to assume they were empty as a couple of thousand pounds of fuel were unusable. This gave us about 10 minutes flying time to spare so we could only make one additional traffic pattern before running out of fuel.

KC-135 refueling fighter aircraft

In 1968, during another Young Tiger sortie flown out of Takli, Thailand, the lead tanker in our flight went into North Vietnam to pickup an F-105 that had been hit and was losing fuel. While he went for the F-105 we refueled the fighters he was originally assigned. Just as the F-105 was about 100 feet from the tanker the engine flamed out (ran out of fuel). The tanker pilot immediately took manual control of his airplane so he could go into a descent to match the F-105s descent. The Boom Operator talked the Tanker pilot back into the refueling position of the fighter. They hooked up and the tanker started to off load fuel into the fighter. The F-105 was able to get the engine started again but couldn't retain the fuel. They stayed hooked up until arriving over Takli AB, Thailand where the F-105 was stationed. The pilot happened to be the Squadron Commander of the Unit and later nominated the Tanker crew for the Air Force Cross. But when word got out that the tanker went into North Vietnam to save the F-105, Strategic Air Command filed article fifteen (court-martial) paperwork on the pilot. When Tactical Air Command found this out they made an issue out of it and the tanker crew ended up being awarded an Air Medal. *If I hadn't contacted Hepititus in Pilot Training, I probably would have been one of those F-105 pilots. I wonder if I could have made it through alive if that happened.*

A typical mission during this tour was to fly in 64 airplane gaggles, where we would have four formation cells of tankers in trail and each tanker would have four fighters assigned for refueling. We would top them off just before they would enter Loas and would wait for them to come back out after they had dropped their bombs in North Vietnam. The hard part was when only 50-70 percent of them would come back.

When I returned from the Young Tiger tour in 1968, I was ready to take my check ride to certify as an aircraft commander. I passed the check ride to become the youngest pilot to become aircraft commander qualified in Strategic Air Command. The Wing Commander asked me which one of the five co-pilots I wanted to fly with. They were all getting out of the Air Force to join the Airlines and outranked me by 3-4 years. He didn't like it when I told him I didn't want any of them as they weren't dedicated and that I wanted to have 2nd lieutenant Gary Kibler assigned as my co-pilot. The problem was Gary had two article fifteens for driving while intoxicated and the Colonel was trying to kick him out of the Air Force. I asked the Colonel to give him another chance and that I thought I could straighten him out and make a productive pilot out of him. The Colonel told me if he ever made a mistake he would kick him out of the Air Force and ruin my career at the same time. I took him anyway. The Navigator assigned to me was Major Cliff Shiers who had just come from a Standardization Crew in the Central Evaluation Group at a base in Louisiana. I was also assigned a senior Boom Operator. We were one of the sharpest crews in the Squadron and I was awarded the Officer of the Year for Strategic Air Command as a result of our crews' performance.

The only close call we had was while on Alert one week the Inspector General's team landed for an Organizational Readiness Inspection. Gary and I were in the Gym playing basketball when the "alert horn" rang. We jumped in the truck and went directly to the airplane. We had problems getting one engine started and were one of the last aircraft to start engines. Another aircraft didn't get their engines started so I knew if I didn't get to the runway threshold in time we would fail the inspection. The Crew Chief we had was new and because he was messing with the engine to get it started he forgot to pull the chocks. When I pushed the throttles up the aircraft wouldn't move. The Crew Chief yelled that he would go back out and pull the chocks. I knew if we did that we would be late, so I pushed the throttles up to full thrust and jumped the chocks. We even cut a 90 degree turn too sharp which put us in the sod area. I got the speed up to over 50 knots and caught the last airplane just as he crossed the threshold giving us a passing reaction time.

The real problem came when we returned to the ramp. An Inspector came to the aircraft to ask us some conditional questions (we called it interrogation). They asked my co-pilot, Gary, how he would put the "Gold Goggles" on if he was at 35,000 feet altitude and he was going into a nuclear war zone. This meant that he would already have his helmet on and would have to put the "Gold Goggles" on over the helmet. He opened the package with the "Gold Goggles" and pulled the strap over his helmet. We thought everything went well.

We got a surprise the next morning when we got off alert to get crew rest for the flight that night. The Squadron Commander Marty Klena, came to the crew bus, got in and pull me out of the bus and said bring your co-pilot and explain why you failed the alert exercise (I thought this was the end of my career!). When we arrived in the Wing Commander's office, the whole Inspector General team, Wing Staff and Squadron Leaders were there waiting to see what we would do. The Wing Commander had the Inspector General on the speaker phone to ask us to go over the situation the co-pilot was asked in the aircraft right after the alert. I went over the situation and told them what the co-pilot did. The Colonel then asked me if I agreed with the way he donned the "Gold Goggles". I told them that I didn't see anything wrong with what he did. The Colonel then said "were you aware the regulation doesn't address putting the "Goggles" on that way and that they should have snapped on the two snaps on our helmet". I responded with "I wasn't aware that there was only one way to don the "Gold Goggles" and still didn't see anything wrong with what he had done as an example what would he do if one of the snaps were missing or damaged so the strap wouldn't fit?". I suggested they change the regulation to include this procedure. The Wing Commander asked the Inspector General if he would consider that and he said he would look into it.

The Squadron Commander, responsible for Crew Training, was so mad he couldn't stand it and stormed out of the room to query all the crewmembers on alert to see if they knew the procedure. Luckily only half of them knew so the Inspection Team failed the training area instead of us. This didn't make the Squadron Commander too happy though the co-pilot and myself survived a "career limiting" situation.

Even after this situation, I was selected as Junior Officer of the Year by Strategic Air Command and was selected as one of 50 Junior Officers to attend the Air Force Association National Convention in Houston, Texas to discuss and come up with solutions for several issues driving hundreds of officers out of the Air Force. I attended a meeting on Rated Pilot Assignments given by Col. English who briefed that anyone could volunteer for a fighter assignment in Viet Nam. I was sitting next to a pilot from the Military Airlift Command (MAC) who had told me they wouldn't let the pilots from MAC volunteer for fighters which was my experience with the Strategic Air Command (SAC). I raised my hand and told the Colonel of our experience and he said it wasn't true. He invited us to the front after the briefing and asked what aircraft we wanted to fly. He gave us a list of airplanes that we could pick from so I gave him a list starting with the F-105, F-4, A-37, F-104, etc. The rest of the conference was great as it gave me a chance to meet with all the Astronauts, Barry Goldwater, Bob Hope and several 2, 3 and 4 star generals. A fraternity brother of mine, Larry Rider, was the escort officer for Barry Goldwater so I was able to talk to him quite a long time.

About a month after returning to K.I. Sawyer AFB, I received a message from the Military Personnel Center that announced my assignment to an A-37 Squadron in Viet Nam. So I was on my way to the Viet Nam War in a fighter. Although it wasn't supersonic, it dropped bombs and strafed. Then about 30 days after this, Colonel English called me personally and said that my assignment had been changed. He said that I hadn't volunteered formally for Vietnam, and therefore couldn't get the A-37 assignment. After telling him that I really was a volunteer, but couldn't formally fill out the paperwork with out the squadron commander giving me a low efficiency rating, he said he would see what he could do.

Two weeks later, he called and told me he had an assignment to OV-10s as a Forward Air Controller and that I would really like it. I didn't know what a Forward Air Controller did, but I was ready to try it. Anything to get out of SAC. After all, I was a fighter pilot at heart.

Just after returning from the Air Force Association Conference, on February 26, 1969, Richard Neal Pumroy was born, and he was the boy I had always wanted (though I loved my daughters as much, a boy is special to a father). Again, I was on alert, only this time I was at Goose Bay, Labrador, Canada to execute our Wartime mission in case of a Nuclear War. This duty was in an underground facility and lasted a week. Of course, Mom Pumroy was there to help Mary with the baby and other kids until I got off alert.

A couple of things made me hesitate in making the decision to volunteer for the Southeast Asia Assignment. First, it is always hard to leave your family for a couple of months, as I already had several times, but this was for a year and there was the possibility that I might not return alive to enjoy seeing the kids grow up. Second, the squadron already had one pilot, Charlie Griffin, who had gone to Southeast Asia flying an OV-10 pilot and was killed in action a couple of months before I received my assignment. But I knew I would have to go eventually, so this was as good a time as any. After a lot of deliberation and prayer, I decided to press on with this new assignment.

CHAPTER SIX
Transitioning to be a FAC

My profile fit a lot of Forward Air Controllers (FACs) from 1969 - 1974. Strategic Air Command and Military Airlift Command had agreed to send their pilots to fighter type aircraft for one year assignments to Viet Nam as they were running short of fighter pilots. This was a big change in the policy from the previous years when the commands would only send pilots to fly conventional aircraft so they could get them back in one year. eight months prior to reporting to Viet Nam, I received orders to report to Cannon AFB, NM to attend a 3 month (90 day fighter pilot wonder school) flying the AT-33 for familiarization in delivering weapons (bombs, rockets and strafing). We were given one week of Ground School which consisted of performance capability and safety procedures for the AT-33 (a T-33 trainer with T-38 engines). The next week after we were taught to taxi the aircraft, we were cleared for some solo training flights in the pattern as the AT-33 only had one seat. After an ordinance class which taught us the capability of various ordinances used in Viet Nam, we were cleared fly missions into the Whiteman Range to practice strafing, dropping 500 pound bombs and

Two OV-10 aircraft flying in formation during training at Hurlburt Field, Florida in Jan 1970.

33

practice shooting rockets. After a little over 50 hours of flight time we were actually getting pretty good at finding and hitting the targets. The only incident we had was when one of the upcoming FACs (Now a medial doctor - name withheld to protect his reputation) bit one of the other pilot's wife, Paula, on the rear end during a get together one evening. We had a close group but that got a little too close. All was forgiven though and a good time was had. Next the same group reported to a 3 month Forward Air Controller (FAC) school in Ft. Walton Beach, Florida flying OV-10's to learn the responsibilities of a FAC. The first 2 or 3 weeks consisted of OV-10 ground school and Air Liaison Officer School. We flew over 50 hours flying simulated Forward Air Controller missions consisting of strafing, bombing and launching white phosphorus rockets and directing simulated strikes using other OV-10 aircraft as the combat aircraft for striking the targets. The OV-10 was an excellent aircraft for the FAC as it was maneuverable, had great visibility and had armored plating in the bottom to protect the pilot. The daily routine was to fly a sortie, meet at Bacons by the Sea for raw oysters and beer and get ready for the next day. Again we had no aircraft incidents but everyone was starting to anticipate what it would be like in actual combat and the wives were starting to realize they would not see their mate for at least a year and maybe never.

It was now February 1970, and I was due to arrive in Viet Nam by mid March. Enroute to Viet Nam I had to attend the 3 week Jungle Survival School at Clark AFB, Philippines. After a short survival course we were positioned in the jungle by helicopter. We spent the next 3 days in the jungle learning first hand how to survive. We ate snake, edible plants and rain water collected in the tree leaves. The last night we were simulating an escape and avoid condition. I had split off from the rest of the group and hid under some fallen bamboo trees. The Air Force hired Nigreto Indians to search and find us. They would receive $5 for every person they found. I was buried under the bamboo and about 2 or 3 o'clock in the morning could hear something approaching me. I laid there waiting and it finally was close enough to put pressure on my leg. I thought it was one of the Negrito Indians, so when I felt the pressure on my leg I raised up real quick to at least scare him as he was about to get rewarded. To my surprise it was a "Pack Rat" about 8 or 9 inches tall and 12 to 15 inches long. I didn't know who it scared most – the Rat or me!

At sunrise, I quietly trekked back to the awaiting helicopter at the rescue point without being found by the Nigreto Indians. This saved the government $5.00 and gave me bragging rights over the others who had gotten caught.

The next stop was Ben Hoa, South Viet Nam for a 3 week indoctrination course. The Base hadn't been mortared for a couple of months, but on our first night the North Vietnamese decided to welcome the new FACs by putting a couple of mortars just outside our barracks. One landed just outside my room with a loud explosion. It woke me up in a panic and as trained immediately put my helmet on and grabbed my M-16 rifle. We were supposed to go directly to the underground bunkers when under attack but since they seemed to have that area zeroed in, so I decided to stay in my room and sleep under the bed the rest of the night. This was enough to scare the crap out of a country boy like me. I had a lot of dangerous experiences but hadn't been shot at before, and I didn't like it.

After experiencing the night life of sleeping through mortar attacks under the bed with an M-16 and a helmet on, I decided I would rather spend my combat experiences getting shot at during the day in an airplane and not at night on the ground, so I volunteered to fly out of Nakon Phanom (NKP), Thailand with the NAIL FACs - I became NAIL 21. I didn't

23ʳᵈ TASS Squadron sign at Nakon Phanom AB, Thailand

realize the next year would be packed with action and flying the best mission in the Air Force at the time. We flew over the Ho Chi Minh trail most every day where there were an average of over 1500 guns every Kilometer along the trail. We averaged about one aircraft shot down per month though we managed to get all but 8 of our fellow pilots out over the year. We had intel that the NVA had a $10,000 bounty on our heads dead or alive which meant we got shot at every flight we flew over Laos. One of the capabilities our OV-10s had over the in-country birds was that we carried four 7.62 MM guns with 2000 rounds and had High Explosive rockets to go with our Willy Petes. The 7.62 MM (mini) guns were mainly for keeping the enemy heads down during search and rescue missions as we were the on-scene commanders of search and rescue missions and needed the means to keep the enemy away from the crewmen until the rest of the rescue team got there. We also used the mini guns for the Prairie Fire mission, when the Heavy Hook team was discovered and the enemy was trying to over take them. The High Explosive rockets were for destroying trucks when we had them pinned in; though we had to be careful of being trapped in a situation where we were too low and surrounded by multiple gun placements.

By now, I was starting to realize that I might have a passion for living on the edge. The rest of my tour as a FAC fed this passion and drove me to volunteer for all the special missions that came my way.

On 28 April 1970, I was assigned a mission to find and destroy some key gun positions that had shot down one of our aircraft earlier in the week. It was along the Ho Chi Minh trail where the river flowed in parallel with the trail. We were pretty sure they had radar

Picture of Ho Chi Minh Trail with bomb craters along both sides of the Trail taken in the Fall of 1970 with a 35 MM Pentax camera from an OV-10 on a combat mission.

directed guns as accurate as they were becoming. When I arrived over the area the weather was marginal with a low layer of clouds with a few sucker holes here and there. The gunners must have thought they were safe as they would fire on me right through the holes in the clouds. What they didn't know was, we had lasers aboard which guided the two thousand pound bombs to the target. I knew where one gun placement was so I ordered up two Wolf Pack fighters (the ones with the guided bombs). They arrived and I had to wait for the clouds to move out from over the area before beaming the target. When the timing was right I pointed the laser cross hair to where I thought the gun placement was and cleared Wolf Pack one in hot. He dropped the first bomb and it hit right on target! We could see it had hit the center vehicle which was the radar vehicle and uncovered the four or five 37MM guns tied into it. I said "Shit Hot Wolf Pack, you hit dead Center and uncovered Pandora's box". However, when the bomb hit target all hell broke loose. It looked like a fourth of July fireworks finale only we were in the middle of the explosions. Four more gun placements started to fire at us. There was a mixture of 23MM, 37MM and 57MM guns. I yelled in the radio "We must have hit a hornets nest and pissed off the whole world; you guys ready to go to work on taking out the rest of them?" Wolf Pack came back saying "we're ready Nail 21, just mark them and we will take them out. I called ABCCC and ordered up some more fighters with guided bombs and we took out the gun placements one at a time. When we were through we destroyed four gun batteries and silenced a number of others. This mission was hairy enough that I received the Distinguished Flying Cross as a recommended by the Wolf Pack pilots.

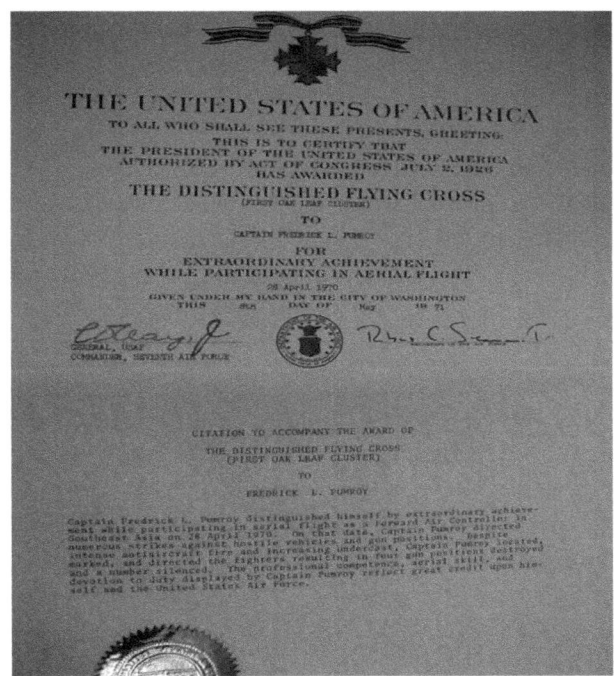

DFC awarded for the mission flown by Fredrick L. Pumroy on 28 April 1970 for directing numerous air strikes against hostile vehicles and gun positions resulting in four gun positions destroyed and a number silenced

During the third month of my FAC tour, I flew with Air America out of UDORN, Thailand to cover for the mission previously flown by the in-country "Raven FACs". The Ravens consisted of FAC pilots, mostly out of the 23rd (TASS), who would put their commission on hold while flying missions under the control of the Central Intelligence Agency (CIA). They actually lived in Laos and flew Porter and T-28 aircraft in support of the Laotian military. Five of the Raven's were killed in one week and it took about 6 weeks to train a new Raven FAC for the mission. So we painted an OV-10 plain with no markings and I locked up my I.D. and moved in with the Air America pilots at Udorn, Thailand. We supported General Van Pow's mission in Laos. This was a low altitude mission with lots of strafing and intelligence gathering.

During one of my missions in support of Air America as a Raven FAC, I was flying cover for some Laotian ground troops at very low altitudes (100 to 1000 feet). I kept seeing what looked like bugs flying past the wind screen. I couldn't figure out what it was until I heard the sound of bullets hitting the side of the aircraft and realized it was AK-47 and 50 Caliber bullets. Needless to say I jinked (changing heading and altitude to avoid enemy tracking) a little faster from then on. I only received about 80 bullet holes that mission according to the crew chief. I had a deal with the crew chief; I would fly the mission and after landing go directly to the Air America bar while he would fix the bullet holes and get the aircraft ready for the next days flight.

On 7 June 1970, in coordination with Air America pilots, I flew a mission deep into a designated anti-aircraft high threat area to conduct air strikes against hostile supply vehicles and a convoy of combat troops. I found the convoy which had a couple of hundred troops; some on foot, some on horses and others in trucks. There was also in excess of 20 supply trucks. I didn't have any fighters assigned to the mission, but did find two T-28s in the area. I was not sure who they were but they were willing to take on the convoy. I didn't have to mark the target as the convoy was out in the open and didn't know we were there yet. I told the T-28 pilots to follow my lead and I would start strafing the convoy with my mini guns while they took out the lead truck. Nothing happened until I started my strafing run and the whole area lit up with small arms fire. I jinked and strafed all the way along the convoy. When I pulled up to take a look at the damage I saw the first truck go up in flames. We made more passes in varying directions and destroyed another truck. When our ordinance was expended and fuel got low, I radioed to ABCCC that we had a convoy blocked and to tell the closest Nail FAC to come over and finish them off. I received another Distinguished Flying Cross and some more bullet holes for this exciting experience. During my two months of flying out of Udorn my aircraft took 309 bullet holes mostly 50 Caliber. This was still a piece of cake when compared to the 23MM, 37MM and 57MM weapons we experienced each day over the Ho Chi Minh Trail.

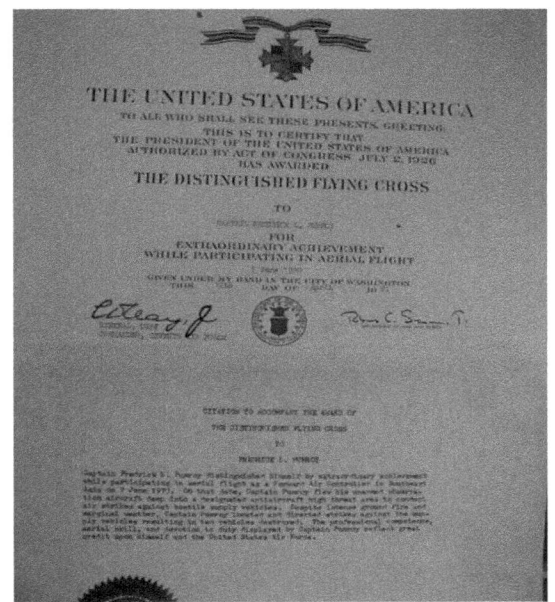

DFC awarded to Fredrick L. Purmroy for mission flown on 7 Jun 1970 during which he flew into a designated high antiaircraft high threat area to conduct air strikes against hostile vehicles resulting in two vehicles destroyed.

Next was the peaceful part of my tour. I was selected by the 23 TASS commander to be the forward operating location (FOL) commander of a unit fling reconnaissance missions over Cambodia. My call sign was Zipgun 21. We had to set up operations out of U-Tapao, Thailand, which was a familiar place for me. I had spent two tours there in the Strategic Air Command flying KC-135s. In fact, my old wing commander at K.I. Sawyer, Brigadier General John Hinton, was just selected as wing commander at U-Tapao. This made it easier for me to set up operations, as we were able to have our own approaches, HF (high frequency) radios, access to the photo lab, and also enjoy air conditioning courtesy of the wing commander.

Picture of a truck in Western Cambodia

Since I was the Operating Location commander, I always took the first flight that way I could observe what was going on during the entire day and not worry about getting ready to fly. I had "Doc" Roberts fly the second sortie and we had a routine of changing positions over a train full of refugees which ran from Cambodia to Thailand the same time every morning. We would fly on opposite sides of the train just high enough to see each other

Picture of a Vietnamese hut taken with a Pentax camera from Fred Pumroy's OV-10 flying along a river in Cambodia

and when we would get abeam of each other we would do a "roll" to the other side. Sometimes it would cause someone to fall off the train as they thought our OV-10s might hit the train.

We covered the western half of Cambodia, mostly taking pictures from our hand-held 35mm cameras and assisting the Cambodian military in finding North Vietnamese (NVA). We flew low-level altitudes, sometimes too low. One picture I took was from ground level into the back end of a Pepsi Cola truck to see what they were carrying. It ended up being armed Cambodian troops - luckily, they were friendly. We also flew down riverbeds below tree canopy level (that cover all but about 100 feet of clear space down the middle of the rivers). We found several NVA camps on the riverbanks using a 35mm Pentax camera and a grease pencil mark on the canopy at an airspeed of 100 knots. This was an antiquated approach but effective. The NVA weren't too happy that we were discovering their location, and they began shooting at us. Luckily, they weren't very good shots.

My most memorable flight out of Utapao was on 4 July 1970, I had spent the early evening at a USO birthday party sponsored by the Wing Commander which served leftover Italian food from the NCO club, since I had the first flight the next morning I didn't have anything to drink "of course". When I woke up I had the G.I.s but decided I could handle it. I arrived at the squadron to find out a 2nd Lieutenant Intel Officer wanted to ride along (it was his first flight in any small airplane). We took off and during our climb over the first mountain range I started to get fierce cramps, so I tried to let the gas out though it was a little juicy. I asked the

Lt. if he had ever flown before and he said "no", so I showed him how to keep the bird straight and level in case I had any more severe cramps at low level (we usually flew at 500 – 1,000 feet). Well I started getting more cramps and you guessed it – I crapped my pants. I started to turn back home but a Cambodian out of Battam Bang called and gave us a message from the Cambodian President – it read something like this: "This day, your independence day, we the people of Cambodia are being invaded and fired upon by the enemies of North Vietnam and to survive we need your bombs to keep them out of our country…..". Then he gave us some coordinates to check out as the NVA were shelling a small town to the East of their position.

We took a look and sure enough about 50 NVA were shelling a small town from a fence row about a half mile away. Of course we couldn't strafe them "Officially", but made a couple of low passes which for some reason made them run from their position. By now we had been out there for about 3 hours with a flight suit full of shit and a very sick Lt in the back seat, I flew back to base and raised the canopy as soon as possible after landing the aircraft. The only thing that kept me going was I kept thinking of my son, Rick, who ran around the yard with a diaper full of crap for hours while playing. If he could do it his dad, Zip Gun 21, could do it! When I parked the aircraft and chalked in, the crew chief saluted and started to come up the ladder. I told him to "get me two ropes" but the crew chief couldn't understand me until he poked his head into the cockpit to un-strap the now embarrassed Zip Gun 21. As he turned white I said "now that you know I shit my pants will you get me two ropes?" The crew chief couldn't find any rope so he took his shoe laces off and handed them to me so I could tie my pant legs at the knee to keep the remainder of the juices from running down my legs. The Lieutenant did the debriefing while I went to my trailer to take a 30 minute shower. My parachute never did get all the smell out of it!!

In August, when I returned to NKP from UTAPAO, now Nail 21 again, I was checked out as an instructor pilot, performing Stan/Eval functions and teaching the new pilots the ins and outs of the Ho Chi Minh Trail, how to strafe, find targets and direct the air strikes. Dennis Crouch and I were the OV-10 evaluators and we were also roommates. Denny and I had the privilege of flying some sorties in formation with official Air Force photographers in each aircraft taking moving pictures of each other putting in air strikes to document the FAC mission. We will probably see these in a war movie one of these days. Our routine day was to fly, debrief, lay out in the sun reflecting on the day, starting a fire to cook Australian steaks and boil dehydrated shrimp, have a couple of 6 ounce glasses of gin or vodka for 15 cents each and go to bed to get ready for the next day. Occasionally we would have a party and end up doing "Dead Bug" (the last one to fall of his chair backwards would have to buy the drinks for all) or "Carrier Landings" (the pilot would land on his belly after getting a running start and would slide the length of an 8 foot plank coated with beer to make it slippery – if the landing was good two other pilots would catch his legs with a rolled up table cloth - if not a good landing they would let the pilot fly right off the end of the plank).

We had certain pilots who earned unwanted nicknames. An Example was "Ducky Wright..

Lt Wright had a bad day as the squadron had lost one of our pilots and he was on the search and rescue team during that day. He was downing several vodkas at the bar where someone had placed a baby duck belonging to another squadron's mascot. The baby duck kept drinking out of his glass and Lt. Wright "talking to the duck", told it not to touch his drink again or he would bite it's head off. Well obviously not able to understand, the little duck took another drink out of the glass and Lt Wright picked it up and bit its head off spitting it on the floor. After looking at his bloody hand he passed out. So one of the other pilots and I picked now "Ducky" Wright up and put him to bed. We also placed the duck next to his face so when he would wake up he would see what he had done. The next morning he woke up seeing the duck and threw up all over the sheets. Earning him the name "Ducky" Wright.

During this time I was checked out in the Prairie Fire mission who supported the Special Forces Heavy Hook operation. On the Prairie Fire mission we carried a Special Forces Heavy Hook rider in the back seat and would checkout the team which had infiltrated the enemy's front line. There would be one Special Forces Warfighter with 6-8 North Vietnam deserters and they would hide in the jungle sabotaging trucks and capturing the enemy to gain intelligence (can't tell you any more of their mission or we would have to kill you). The Prairie Fire mission was to fly cover for the Heavy Hook teams that were on the ground and to find insertion points. This was a low altitude mission flown at tree top levels and over highly populated enemy territory. The trick was to fly over the Heavy Hook locate to determine their status without letting the enemy know where they were located.

The mission wasn't too dangerous unless the Heavy Hook team location was compromised, and we had to execute an extraction. Then we would lay it on the line and do what it took to keep the enemy from overrunning the Team. This usually meant taking several hits from small arms such as AK-47 and 50 Caliber Guns. This would happen about once every other month, but we didn't loose any of the Heavy Hook Team leaders during my time with them.

On one of the missions I was scheduled for but couldn't fly, Bill Sanders took my place with Al Mosiello in the back seat. While over the Ho Chi Minh trail they got hit by a Stella shoulder held missile. Bill was killed instantly and Al ejected and was successfully rescued. Though I knew this wasn't my fault, I have always felt guilty that it wasn't me flying that airplane. Their mission is described in the FAC Book.

On another Prairie Fire mission, Al Mosiello (my Special Forces Heavy Hook rider in the rear seat) and I went on our usual low level observation flight to check out the Special Forces team on the ground in the mountain range just north of the Ho Chi Minh trail. Al had established contact with the Team using the secure radio. The team had been discovered by the North Vietnamese and was under attack. Al told me over inter-com that we needed to called-in some ordinance. I called ABCCC over the radio: "'Sky King' do you have any fighters for us today? We have some friendlies being overrun". ABCCC came back with "Nail 21, I don't have anything prog'd for an hour".

We contacted the special forces rescue team back at NKP to come to our rescue, so they were on there way. In the mean time we contacted an Air America T-28 and asked him to come over and help. The Air America pilot checked in and we briefed him where the Team was and where the Viet Cong were on the mountain side. We told the Air America pilot we would take the lead and for him to follow. So we rolled in and strafed the NVA's position with our 50 caliber machine guns to keep the enemy from overrunning the Team's position until we could get some fighter aircraft with napalm bombs to neutralize the bad guys. After about 30 minutes, ABCCC found some aircraft with napalm and they checked in. We had kept the Viet Cong from getting closer with our 50 Caliber machine guns, now it was time to take them out. We cleared the F-4s in one at a time using napalm. It took us about 20 minutes to get the napalm dropped and the rescue team to get the Heavy Hook team safely out. Four A-1Es and one rescue helicopter from NKP arrived for the extraction. The team was able to bring some of the NVA back with them to interrogate for more information. The Heavy Hook team had been out in the field for more than 10 days and was happy to get back with only a few wounds.

I went to Bangkok with this team and stayed at the Special Forces hotel (Roma Hotel). Only Special Forces and associates stayed there for a good reason. What went on at the hotel stayed at the hotel. For example, one night we were having a few beers reminiscing about some of our missions when one of the guys missed his "girl friend for the night" and one of the guys with him told him she had gone upstairs with another Special Forces troupe. He immediately got up and went to his room to find it locked from the inside. Realizing his Special Forces buddy and his girl friend were in his room using the chair they had rigged up for sexual activities. He pulled out his pistol and shot the lock open. Went into the room and picked the girl and the chair she was in up and threw both out the third story window. The girl and chair both survived as they landed in the hotel pool. When we got back from the R & R trip, Capt Mike Taylor, one of their commanders told him he was lucky the pool was there to catch the girl. The Special Forces soldier responded with "what pool"?

Another occasion that demonstrated the attitude of the Heavy Hook soldier was when we invited them into the NKP Officers Club for dinner one night. The Club had Kobe beef on the menu and a stripper for entertainment. As we entered the dining room a 2nd Lieutenant was having dinner alone and was eating a thick juicy Kobe steak. One of the Heavy Hook Sergeants went over and asked the Lieutenant how his steak was and before he could answer the Sergeant picked the steak up with his hands and took a big bite out of it and said "hey, this is a great steak, glad you recommended it", put the steak back on the plate, walked over to our table, sat down and ordered a Kobe steak for himself. The Lieutenant didn't say a word, just finished his meal and left.

The Prairie Fire pilots and Heavy Hook warfighters also had a special "CIA approved identification card" and a black jeep that all security police both civilian and military knew and recognized. So, occasionally we would stray across the Thailand/Laotian border to experience the night life and buy gold on the Laotian side of the river. If the Air Force would have found out we would have been burnt toast. But it gave us the freedom to roam the country that no other organization had except the Air America employees and CIA agents themselves.

Some of the FAC pastimes included games like "Dead Bug", "Carrier Landings", and "Last to Dane on the Bar" to determine who would buy the next round of drinks. When someone yelled "Dead Bug" the last person to fall off their chair backwards and hit the floor would buy the drinks. Carrier Landings required more planning to execute: You would put beer on a 10 foot table or plank, two pilots would twist a table cloth so that when the pilot doing the Carrier Landing dove on the table from a running start they would catch his legs which should have been in a perpendicular position keeping him from flying off the end of the table or plank (of course if the pilot made a bad landing or approach they would lift the table cloth and he would fly off the end of the table on to the floor). When someone would yell "last to dance on the bar", everyone would climb up on the bar and flail around (the last one up on the bar bought the drinks). Though these were childish games it kept our minds off the events of the day which included being shot at and sometimes hit, losing an aircraft occasionally along with one of your fellow pilots or a near miss with one of the fighters we were controlling.

The Squadron lost an average of one aircraft per month, but only lost 8 of the pilots during our year tour. Overall during the war 64 OV-10 aircraft were lost with 43 fatalities and 5 prisoners of war (POWs), 102 O-2 aircraft with 84 fatalities and 2 POWs and 178 O-1s were lost with 93 fatalities and 1 POW.

Some of the other missions we were involved in included: the Prairie Fire mission in support of the then classified "Heavy Hook" program; on-scene commander for Search and Rescue missions; implanting "Sensors" for the "Igloo White" program on major roadways going into North Vietnam; the "Pave Way" program - operating hand held laser beams to guide the two & three thousand pound Pave Way bombs on target; flying reconnaissance missions over Western Cambodia by our flight out of Utapao, Thailand under the call sign of "Zip Gun"; and flying reconnaissance missions over Eastern/Northern Cambodia by our flight flying out of UBON, Thailand with the call sign of SPIKE (one of them will tell their story).

My experience in combat was one that gave me great insight into my personal strengths and weaknesses, but I wouldn't want to have to do it again. *I was not sure how many more tough fixes God would get me out of.*

45

CHAPTER SEVEN
Assignment to Hawaii

My initial assignment to Hawaii was in the "Blue Eagle" Airborne Command Post Squadron. The qualifications to just be a co-pilot was to have 2500 total flying hours and be Aircraft Commander qualified. With my FAC time I just had over the required 2500 hours and was selected. All the other co-pilots were Majors and the Aircraft Commanders were Lt. Colonels who were instructor qualified.

The first requirement was to get re-qualified in the aircraft. The unit had a waiver to check out their own pilots so I was checked out on the job to include how to take-on fuel as a receiver pilot in both seats. Within six months I was selected as the Stan Eval Copilot. This upset the other co-pilots since I had just gotten there and was still a Captain.

Shortly after my selection as a standardization evaluation co-pilot, our crew was selected to fly Admiral McCain, CINCPAC and his battle staff while he received a new airplane which had fan engines which was a great deal more powerful than the "Water Wagons" we had been flying. During the next six months his crew was permanently reassigned and he selected our crew to take their place. Now we had a "Hot" new airplane and now we were looking forward to flying all over the world in it.

We flew the Admiral to every Navy base in the Pacific at least twice a year. That meant we flew into Guam, Okinawa, Philippines, Taiwan, Hong Kong, Australia, Bali Beach, Singapore, Diego Garcia, Thailand, Korea and Johnston Island. Each location had its unique qualities and our crew enjoyed experiencing them all. A typical lay over would be for two or three days.

We had two pilots, a navigator, a load master, an engineer, a flight steward and a radio operator. The airplane had wall-to-wall carpeting, hot and cold running water, a four burner oven, ice chest, and china dishware. The Admiral had an apartment in the rear of the aircraft which housed himself, his wife and her sister. Our activities included drinking a beer or two on the way to the hotel, having horsduerves made

Figure 1: C-135 in front of terminal at Hickam AFB, Hawaii. Used to transport the Commander in Chief of the Pacific Forces in the early 1970s

by the stewards, setting up a bar in the navigator and my hotel sweet, organizing the itinerary for the next stay which usually included tennis and golf.

Most of our missions were uneventful except for a few. Flying into Hong Kong was always a thrill as there was no instrument approach to the runway. You had to navigate to a small island just outside Hong Kong using an Air Directional Finder (ADF) instrument (which we didn't have on our aircraft). So we had to visually navigate using precision maps and the navigator's radar. Once you found the small island they had lights on top of the buildings, guiding traffic to a 90 degree approach leg, then a 45 degree leg then final approach.

On the last flight we had into Hong Kong it was raining so it was hard seeing the landmarks and lights. Luckily we had been in there a couple of times so we knew where we were most of the time and knew about how far from the mountains to fly to keep the approach lights in sight. We lost sight of the lights several times, but somehow we made it on to final approach and landed without incident.

During a trip to Korea, we were visiting Kunsan AB when the North Koreans broke though the Demilitarized Zone (DMZ). It was enough of a threat that the Admiral told us we needed to depart immediately. The problem was the gusty cross wind was about five knots over our cross wind component for takeoff. We informed the Admiral we couldn't takeoff legally because of the wind. He asked what the danger was if we did try. We told him we had never taken off in such a condition but probably could if we pulled back the outboard throttle of the down wind engine. He said give it a go as the North Koreans were targeting the base we were visiting.

We took off with me in the co-pilot seat and control of the throttles. As we accelerated down the runway the aircraft started to skid to the right into the wind. I slowly pulled back the left engine to keep us on the runway and the pilot had full rudder in. Just as we approached the edge of the runway we had enough speed to rotate and just made it off the ground before going into the grass.

The next mission wasn't as dangerous but was unique. We were flying to Thailand when we received a call from the Secretary of Defense on the "HF" radio that the United States was being offered a gift from Lon Noll the President of Cambodia and the Admiral was supposed to officially meet with him and accept the gift. The gift was a "White Bull" elephant. The admiral came up to the cockpit which he did quite often as his wife and her sister wouldn't let him smoke his cigar in their compartment in the back of the airplane. He said "what the HELL are we going to do with a "White Bull" elephant?" We told him we would take care of it. We contacted the Honolulu Zoo but they said in order for them to accept the elephant we would have to put it in quarantine for 6 weeks (what do you do with an elephant for 6 weeks on an Air Force Base?). We ended up calling the Mayor of Los Angeles and he was able to convince the LA Zoo to take the elephant. So we made arrangements to have a C-130 fly into Nom Phen, Cambodia's capital city to pickup the elephant.

It was necessary to sedate the elephant and tie it to several pallets to get it safely into the aircraft. Another Navy aircraft took the Admiral to Cambodia. The C-130 carried the elephant to Bangkok, Thailand and transferred it to a C-141. The C-141 flew the elephant to Los Angeles where it was transported by truck to the LA Zoo.

We arrived in Los Angeles one day before the C-141 and started setting up a ceremony and reception for the California Governor and Los Angeles Mayor to formally accept the elephant. After 3 days glad handing and partying we were ready to return to Hawaii.

On another unique mission, we picked up members of the Southeast Asia Treaty Organization (SEATO) in Bankok, Thailand. Our mission was to fly them to Andrews AFB, Virginia for a meeting at the White House in Washington D.C.. The entire SEATO party flew to Bangkok and were escorted to our aircraft. We departed Bangkok with Lt Col Hess as pilot and flew directly to Elmendorf, Alaska for a refueling stop then I took it on in to Andrews AFB in Virginia. The flight took over 24 hours which was beyond our legal limits as a flight crew. We were supposed to have an extra pilot and navigator, however the Admiral waived the requirement upon our request. Lt Col Hess and I didn't have it too bad as we took turns taking a nap, but Major Beringson, the navigator, wasn't able to sleep until we hit land and we could pick up the navigation aids.

The problem came when we arrived at Andrews AFB to find it closed due to fog. The ceiling was less than one hundred feet. We then diverted to Dulles Airport just West of Washington D.C. but the ceiling was right at 100 feet which was 100 feet below Air Force minimums but was acceptable in the airline industry.

As I flew the approach to minimums, I could barely pickup the threshold lights at 100 feet. I decided to give it a try since there were calm winds and it was easy to maintain the course and glide path. Now we could pick up the runway lights and felt a sigh of relief until I rotated and lost visual contact of all lights until the lowering the nose of the aircraft and luckily we were still on the runway. Our landing speed was approximately 130 knots so it wouldn't have taken much to veer off the course line but we had made it on the ground and came to a slow crawl as we couldn't see more than one runway light ahead and had to be led in by a follow-me truck. This is one of those missions you went directly to bed and thanked God for guiding you through it.

Another unique experience was when my wife Mary and I flew "Space Available" on a C-5 to Kadena AFB, Okinawa and had to be in Bankok in three days. When we arrived at Kadena we were 27th on the list of passengers trying to get to Southeast Asia. Even some of the active duty passengers on the waiting list had been there for 3 or 4 days and the smell was getting pretty rank.

We couldn't get out the first night so the second day I started going in to the weather/flight planning room and talking to the crews. They were transporting engines and supplies which put them on the grey line of whether it would be save to have passengers on-board. I let a Chief Mast Sergeant Load Master know that there were several active duty individuals waiting to go back to the war zone and they should be allowed to get on as passengers. I also let him know I was doing it for selfish reasons as we had to be in Bangkok in two days. He talked to the pilot and came back and told me they were going to release 17 seats and to wait around in case they could release some more.

Seventeen passengers were called to board the aircraft, and those that remained left to get some sleep before the next aircraft came in. About 45 minutes after the first 17 passengers left they announced that they were releasing two more seats. So my assistance in getting the others on paid off as Mary and I were the next two passenger on the list.

As we got out to the C-130 aircraft we realized why they didn't normally release the seats as there were only parachute seats around the side of the aircraft with two engines down the center of the cargo compartment. It was loud and uncomfortable but it was a free ride to Udorn, Thailand which was about a two hour flight and 10 hour drive from Bangkok.

When we landed at Udorn (I had been stationed there for two months flying with Air America) I looked over and the last flight to Bangkok was boarding. So I grabbed Mary by the arm and yelled at the Navy shipman to keep up with me if they wanted to get to Bangkok that night. I flagged down a taxi and told him to "By Layo" to the Air Terminal. When we arrived the airliner was starting engines and I found someone who spoke English and told them we had to get on that airplane as it was an emergency. To my surprise they held the airplane as we got out our American Express credit card to pay and off we went to Bangkok.

We arrived in Bangkok in time to get to the American Embassy where they were holding our tickets and we were now ready for our flight the next morning. We traveled to Taiwan, Hong Kong, and Korea before heading back to Hawaii. We spent 3 days at Korea and when we tried to get on the airline they were over booked so we couldn't get out. The airline put us up over night and served the group a 12 course Korean dinner. We partied all night and met several movie stars who were coming back from cutting a film in China called the "China Caper".

The next morning, I went to the Army base in Seoul to call back to Hawaii and let them know I would be too late to fly a mission I was scheduled to fly with the Admiral's battle staff. They substituted another pilot and told me to take my time getting back as they had me covered. The flight with the Admiral was to Guam then on to Diego Garcia as they were setting up a Navy base there. They landed safely at Diego Garcia but when they took off the water shutdown early and they had to come back and land with a full load of fuel and the engines running at reduced thrust. They were lucky to get it back around and land without blowing tires or having enough thrust to keep the bird in the air. This is another incident I avoided which could have been a disaster. God was looking after me again!

One of my missions during this time still was tied to the Vietnam War. My crew was selected to fly into Saigon to pickup Gen Westmoreland and his staff. The ceremony to give military control back to the South Vietnamese was held just outside our aircraft wing tip. General Westmoreland made a speech and gave the Vietnamese General Ky a symbolic "Key" as he officially transferred military control. This was concurrent with the release of the POWs in 1973. My neighbor Colonel Rich Able was the negotiator of the POW release.

After the transfer of military control General Westmoreland boarded our aircraft with about 10 of his staff and we taxi'd to the end of the runway ready for takeoff. We reached Colonel Able by HF Radio to find the North Vietnamese were refusing to release the prisoners on a technicality.

The General was sitting in the jump seat between us, and after I told him of the delay, he said, Tell those bastards we are not leaving this place until the last POW is off the ground.

The General refused to take off until the last POW was in the air which resulted in two delayed takeoffs over a three day period. When the release was finally agreed to we waited until the last aircraft carrying the POWs were off the ground then we took off. We flew the General to Kadena to stay out of the way of the POWs who were flying to Clark. On the way I heard the call sign HOMECOMING 12345 over the HF radio. They were truly American Heros!

I called him over the radio "HOMECOMING this is Junta 66 (our call sign), do you have Jim Latham aboard? Jim was a NAIL FAC I had checked out in the OV-10, who had come home and returned for a second tour in the F-4 and was shot down early in his second tour. A voice came back stating " Yes, Pumroy I have him in my jump seat". Since I hadn't given him my name I asked who he

Figure 2: Shown here is a veteran visiting the Wall in Washington D.C. to reflect on the loss of some of his fellow warfighters

was. He was Bob Powell another NAIL FAC I flew with at NKP who had volunteered to go in and pick up the POWs. Mary and I met Jim when they flew the POWs to Hawaii for a stop over one morning at about 3:00 A.M. We brought him a lay made of miniature liquor bottles, but they confiscated them and gave them to him later. It was a real honor to meet and greet these fellow pilots who endured so much physical and mental torture.

During one of my last missions into Taiwan I had just received word that I was being reassigned to Wright-Patterson AFB, Ohio as a Special Project Officer to General Jack Catton, Commander of Air Force Logistics Command and I ran into Lt Col Bill Page at the Roma Hotel bar. Bill had medals that reached his lapel as he was the most decorated pilot in the Air Force at the time serving in WWII, Korea and Viet Nam wars. He was also flying T-39 aircraft stationed at Wright-Patterson AFB operated by the 89th Squadron out of Andrews AFB flying dignitaries around the United States.

After exchanging war stories for a couple of hours and telling him I was being assigned to Wright-Patterson AFB, he volunteered to sponsor me when I transferred and would get me into the 89th flying squadron as a rated supplement job.

In September 1973, our crew was selected to pick up General Timothy O'Keefe at McDill AFB to fly him to Nakon Phanom, Thailand where he would be commander of the 7th Air Force. After a night of partying at the general's house, we flew back to Hawaii for a one night stay (the general wanted to stop and see some friends he had made while vice commander of the Pacific Air Forces during his previous assignment). The next day, we took off for Kadena AFB with a fuel stop at Guam. During the flight from Guam to Okinawa, General O'Keefe came up to the cockpit and asked if we would like to play a round of golf with him after we landed. Of course we couldn't refuse an invitation like this, so the radio operator called ahead to make arrangements. To save time, we took turns flying the airplance while the other changed into civilian clothes.

When we landed, the two star general who was the commander of the 13th Air Force met the airplane. On our way out of the aircraft, the wing commander, who was a full colonel, asked who was in charge of the aircraft. We all pointed to our senior master sargeant loadmaster and jumped into the general's staff car, headed for the golf course. The next couple of hours proved to be the fastest round of golf I have ever experienced. The golf course had set up two golf carts with clubs and golf shoes our size, ready to go. The two star general went ahead of us in a golf cart telling the other golfers to let us play through. To save time, we hit the ball when ready. If the ball went into the rough, we would hit from where we thought it went in and continued hitting the ball toward the green. The only time we paused was on every sixth hole – someone would bring us a "Salty Dog" drink (vodka with grapefruit juice).

We finished 18 holes in one and a half hours. At the clubhouse, we had another drink and hors d'oevres. The local commander made reservations for dinner at the local Chinese restaurant on base. We had a great 7-course meal, with all the trimmings. After dinner, we returned to the VIP quarters, where our luggage was waiting. On the way, I was the designated driver and missed the turn because it was pouring down rain. I spun the car around to get back to the street entrance we were supposed to take. General O'Keefe asked what was that and I said it was a "DERF maneuver" (DERF is the nickname he gave me the year prior while flying into Taiwan when he came up to the cockpit and asked how it was going – I had been taking a nap with my head resting on my bracelet which had "FRED" engraved on it-read backward is "DERF", my new nickname).

The next day, it was my turn to fly into Nakon Phanom, where I had landed hundreds to times in an OV-10 Bronco. We arrived early, so I made a couple of circles. I wanted to time an approach so we would taxi in on time for the reception ceremony. Just as I started my turn to final, tower called and informed us that the winds had changed. We now had an eight-knot tailwind and should change runways. If we flew to the other runway, we would be over ten minutes late, so I decided to go ahead and land. What I forgot was that the runway, on the approach end, went downhill the first 3,000 feet. With a tail wind, our airspeed was hot, and the airplane wouldn't settle to the runway.

The general was in the jump seat, so I told him to hang-on. I was easing down the aircraft using the speed brakes. Bottom line – it was the worst landing I had ever made.

CHAPTER EIGHT
Flying a Desk

I arrived at Wright-Patterson AFB in July 1974 and looked up Bill Page as soon as I reported. As promised he was actively flying T-39s for the 89th in support of the Wright-Patterson AFB Commander General Jack Catton and VIPs. General Catton had directed Maj General Buckingham to hire me into his new Acquisition organization. This didn't go over to well as General Buckingham had hand picked all his people except for me and I was the only rated officer. It didn't make it any easier when they found out I was going to be flying part time with the 89th.

The only flight that was exciting during the next two year period was during my initial checkout flight. I knew I was in trouble because my Evaluator was Capt Rickert, who had been a navigator with me when we were stationed at K.I. Sawyer, Michigan together in the late 1960s.. He was selected for Pilot Training and was assigned to Wright-Patterson AFB right out of school. I had given him some hairy flights so he was going to get even.

On the ground he queried me on every minute thing. Then during our initial takeoff he pulled one of the two engines to idle just as I rotated. After going through the emergency procedures, I tried to bring the engine back up but he said I had lost the engine for the rest of the flight. Once in the air he had me change my flight plan to proceed directly to the Cincinnati Airport where we flew an Instrument Landing System (ILS) approach and a radar directed approach. He took the airplane after the second approach and told me to get clearance into the restricted airspace just east of the Cincinnati Airport with a block altitude of 10,000 to 30,000 feet. Once in the area he told me to close my eyes and he rolled the aircraft upside down into a slight dive. He said "this is an unusual attitude recover". I proceeded to go through the procedure for successfully getting out of that particular unusual attitude. He did two more unusual attitudes one out of a "Split S" maneuver and one out of a "Chandelle".

This would not have been so bad except the aircraft was limited to "2.5Gs" (two and a half times earth's force of gravity). He would show me how to do the various acrobatic maneuvers without exceeding the limits of the aircraft. So we both went through each of the maneuvers: Loops, Split S, Barrel Roll, Chandelle, and Stalls. We had one more instrument approach we had planned to do at Springfield Airport, but the instruments were too precessed to make even a non-precision approach so he talked me through a gyro out approach. We made it back without the wings falling off and I was now certified to fly passengers by myself.

In 1976, I was selected to attend the Defense Systems Management College (DSMS). It was a Masters level course over a six month time period. It was like taking in information through a fire hose, but we learned a lot in the short period of time. There were three of us from Wright-Patterson AFB: Tom Honeywell, Tom Harruff and myself. We took turns driving back to Dayton every other month to see our families. The weekends we stayed at Ft. Belvoir, Virginia, we were able to golf and/or play tennis.

When I returned to Wright-Patterson AFB, I was assigned to the original B-1A program as the Chief of the Deployment Division. It was the first time they broke this organization out from Test and gave it to Logistics to manage. The first day on the job I had to write a Request for Proposal for a Facility Plan. The previous facilities

B-1 Bomber on the ground at Edwards AFB getting ready for a Test Flight in 1982. The total program cost was $22.5 billion and the logistics support cost was $2.5 billion that was $500 million short of need

manager had hired a company to do it and had them contract it out to his wife who in turn had the manager himself write the plan. The problem was he was also the approval authority over the plan (a slight violation of

Federal Law). He had a choice of retiring or going to jail. He retired. The plan was completed and I had a good deployment plan developed along with five surveys of the initial basing sites for the B-1A Bomber. However, President Carter decided to cancel the program so now I was out of a job and transitioned to the team which closed the contract except for some residual development tasks.

My next assignment was to the Strategic System Program Office where I was Chief of the Integration Division. There were 26 projects in the Program Office that we were responsible for and I was responsible for integrating the logistics and maintenance support requirements into the development and production programs for each project. After a couple of months I was also selected as the Director of Logistics for the Ground Launch Cruise Missile (GLCM) which was managed out of the Crystal City complex in Washington DC. I would travel to Washington DC or San Diego, California (where the prime contractor was) on Monday and return to Dayton on Thursday night so I could get briefed on what my people had done in the Dayton office on Friday morning. I would then brief General Nick Chubb on all my programs Friday afternoon or Saturday morning. This went on for approximately nine months until I left for Air Command and Staff College in Montgomery Alabama in July 1978. *Talk about overload. I was ready for a break.*

During the last winter at Wright-Patterson AFB we had a near fatal crash in our Volkswagon Bug. I was late for an intramural basketball game on base and had Mary in the front seat with the three kids in the back seat. It had snowed all day with about 4 inches accumulated. We were traveling down a back road in Beavercreek, Ohio where we lived at about 40 miles per hour. The roads had been plowed so they were clear except for about 200 feet where the road dipped just before going over a bridge. The snow plow couldn't get down to the cement at that point so there were roots in the road. As I approached this area, I didn't see the grooves in the road in time and the car started to spin. I stopped the spinning but the car was accelerating backward into the side of the road where there was a bank of snow. The car hit the snow bank and rolled backward over it into the water stream which crossed the road.

The car landed upside down with the car still running. I could smell gas so I shut the car off and looked for the kids. They ended up in the cargo area in back of the back seat and were crying but didn't appear hurt. The next thing I tried to do was get out of the car. The doors were blocked by snow. I proceeded to kick the passenger window in the front seat out and help Mary and the kids get out of the car. The ambulance took us to the base hospital to take x-rays. No one was hurt and the kids only had a few scratches. Mary and I had a strained necks. I have since slowed down in icy weather though Mary still gets anxiety attacks when the weather conditions are icy. *Again, how many lives will God give me?*

In Air Command and Staff College we learned Air Force and Department of Defense war doctrine. In addition I attended the Air Force Comptroller School. One of the neat parts of the school were the people you associated with. In addition to Air Force personnel we had one person from the Army, one from the Navy, one from Bangladesh, and one from Jordan. Zack was from Bangladesh and an Air Force Colonel in charge of maintenance for the entire Bangladesh Air Force. Duar Melkawe was from Jordan and he was a Lieutenant Colonel in the Jordanian Air Force who had been the personal helicopter for the Queen. We entertained both of them and gained great insight into the situations in each of their country.

My wife, Mary, had painted a portrait of Duar's wife Reme. At the end of the school, when Duar was packing for his return, we stopped in to present the painting to Reme and say goodbye. As I watched him pack, I had made a statement that I liked the leather pilots brief case he had. He asked me if I wanted it. I said, 'no I had one of my own that was provided by the Air Force'. He asked me again. I said, 'no I can't take yours, you need it'. He then said "Our custom is if we ask you three times if you would accept a gift then we would not be friends anymore".

Needless to say I accepted and still have the leather bag in my attic. We tried to contact both of them but was unsuccessful and haven't heard from them since.

While at Air Command and Staff College, the Iranians captured 52 American hostages and were holding them in the American Embassy Compound. Strategic Air Command was looking for someone who had special forces experience, receiver air refueling qualified and had flown low level combat missions. Guess who met all the qualifications and was assigned back to Strategic Air Command?

CHAPTER NINE
Iranian Hostage Raid

During Air Command and Staff College, it was announced that I had been promoted to Lieutenant Colonel and had all of these qualifications (Receiver pilot, experienced in low level flying and had worked with the CIA). I was assigned to Grissom AFB, Indiana where I was to develop a training curriculum for receiving fuel from a KC-135 aircraft and offloading fuel to MC/AC 130 aircraft at altitudes below five thousand feet above mean sea level. The problem was I hadn't flown a 135 type aircraft since 1974 and had to go through re-qualification at Castle AFB in Merced California. While there I ran into Lt. General Jim Mullins who was the 15th Air Force Commander stationed at March AFB, California.

I was in my Class A uniform cashing a check at the Officers Club when I saw some people wearing historic uniforms. It appeared they were modeling them in the Ball Room so I peaked in the door to see who they were modeling for and there was General Mullins and the entire Wing staff sitting at the table. The Wing Commander was telling the General a joke or war story when the General looked up and saw me in the door. He ignored the Colonel and stood up motioning me over to the table.

"What are you doing here," he asked.

I told him I was going through re-qualification and instructor upgrade school. He asked me if I would want to go to work for him at 15th headquarters. I told him that my mother-in-law and my father both had cancer and I was getting involved in the Rapid Deployment Force so I wanted to be close to them and train the SAC pilots how to refuel at low altitudes. Both my mother-in-law and father were living in Indiana and both were close to Grissom AFB where we were stationed. This decision probably cost me the chance of getting a promotion to General later.

The biggest thrill I had at Castle AFB was when I ran into an instructor I knew from my previous assignment to SAC and bet him I could refuel a B-52 on the first flight with no practice flying the aircraft itself. He scheduled a flight the next week

Figure 1: RC-135 refueling from a KC-135 over Alaska in 1980 in support of the Alaskan Tanker Task Force

so I could fly with an instructor and make it legal. The rest of that week I was able to get into the B-52 simulator and flew some refueling sorties even though it was nothing like the real thing I could get a feel for the slow response of the B-52.

At the end of the student training flight they had some time so the instructor said to get in and show my stuff. At first I over controlled the aircraft as you would put in a turn of the wheel and nothing would happen for a couple of seconds. So I did "S" maneuvers all the way up the KC-135 tanker. Then I finally got onto the trick of flying a B-52. You would put a correction in and take it out and wait. You had to keep that up until in the position you wanted. I was able to get hooked up on the second try, so I had martini's the rest of the night when we landed. I went back to Grissom all checked out and was selected as the Operations Office for one of the squadrons. Grissom had three types of 135s: KCs (tankers), ECs (Airborne Command Post aircraft) and RTs (receiver tankers).

About a month after returning from Castle, I was sent to Alaska for a month which extended from before Christmas to after New Years. The temperature averaged 60 degrees below zero and 90 degrees below with the chill factor.

One mission we took off on a flight which extended over the North Pole to refuel an RC-135. We had just arrived over the North Pole when the number one engine blew and caught fire. We shut the fuel flow off for that engine and the fire finally went out. We were supposed to abort the mission but were only about 15 minutes from joining with the RC-135, so we went ahead and refueled him with three engines running. I was glad to have started out with four engines at this point as there is no place to land except on a rough bed of ice and no population anywhere in sight. We all wondered how we would survive if we had to crash land in such an isolated area.

Everything went well until we arrived back at the base. They were calling for 100 foot visibility with calm winds. We could see the runway from above but there was ice fog which limited your horizontal vision. What we didn't know was that on top of that there was a wind shear at about 1000 feet just as you went into the fog. The first try I was right on glide path until I went into the fog and the winds quit and before I could take the crab out the ILS course indicator pegged to the right. I initiated a go-around and pulled the outboard engine which was running to idle and flew the next approach with the inboard engines. This time I stayed right of course so when the wind quit I could stay on course as the wind shear occurred. It was still a little testy, since the visibility was less than 100 feet and I could barely see the runway when I rotated during the landing. *Another one for the Almighty!*

Figure 2: AC-130 Gunship used during the Iranian Hostage Raid in 1981. This shows the AC-130 coming in to refuel from our RT-135 practicing for the Hostage Raid

Within six months of returning from Alaska, I was immediately sent to Guam to develop low level refueling tactics receiving fuel from a regular KC-135 and off-loading the fuel to a MC or AC-130 over the water. The SAC pilots hadn't received fuel or off-loaded fuel below 18,000 feet prior to this. The only problem was that the air is more turbulent at low level and you had to contend with birds and other aircraft flying in uncontrolled airspace. Another problem was that when off-loading fuel to the MC or AC-130 aircraft, the tanker's airspeed was about 10 knots below stall speed when refueling these aircraft since they could only accelerate to 190 knots. So when the 130 aircraft would go under the nose of the receiver tanker we would slow down from 270 knots to 190 knots and when the airspeed went through 220 and 210 knots we would lower 20 and 30 flaps respectively. We also had to learn some new techniques of joining up with a regular tanker during the departure climb as we would have to hookup and take on fuel prior to getting to the 130 aircraft. We practiced this procedure for about seven months staging out of several different bases with no support scheduled to practice bare base operations.

We flew these sorties at night with no radar or lights. The MC or AC-130 had an infra-red light on the top of it so we could pick it up with infra-red night goggles. The first incident we had during these practice flights was one night during a mission just south of Las Vegas over the desert one of our tankers joined up with what he thought was an AC-130 but when he pulled up in front of it and the boom operator lowered the boom the "Commercial Airliner" abruptly banked and sped away. We had to have the CIA find the pilot of the Airliner to keep him from filing a formal complaint to FAA about a near miss.

The second incident happened during a takeoff out of Eglin AFB. On takeoff the water on two engines quit so I had to abort the takeoff and taxi back to the takeoff position for another try. The normal procedure was to return to the maintenance area to determine cause and to fill the aircraft up with water. I thought, *Pumroy, do you take a chance on losing water early or not? If you do, you could be killing yourself and three others.*

We didn't have time to do the trouble shooting, so I decided to give it another try since the cause of this was usually due to corrosion on the micro switches for those engines. During the second takeoff, I moved the throttles full forward and backward a couple of times until the water energized on all four engines. The real problem came when the water ran out just after I had raised the gear. Without water we had lost a couple thousand pounds of thrust and the aircraft started to settle. In order to keep the airspeed up I had to lower the nose. By the time I obtained climb speed we were less than a 100 feet above the Bay connecting to the Gulf of Mexico. We flew over several sail boats out for a romantic cruise. It must have given them a scare as I knew I was sweating it out myself.

The first week of April 1981, we were told to pack our bags for 90 days and to fly to Europe to support the Tanker Task Force out of England. Of course we took tennis gear and golf clubs just in case we had some time off. When we arrived in England we were told to check into a hotel in a small town about 15 miles away from the base and to keep in radio contact ready for an immediate deployment. That meant no alcoholic beverages but we were able to play tennis and golf. About 5 days went by when we got the call at around 10:00 P.M. to report to the commander's office. This was the first time we were brief on the mission to rescue the hostages in Iran, although we had expected that this was what we were there for.

There were six aircraft in our Rapid Deployment Tanker Force. France was the only country who wouldn't let us over fly their boundary. To keep them from knowing what we were up to we filed United Airline call signs and flew three two ship wing tip formations filing into Cairo, Egypt. We were instructed to ignore any communication requests or aircraft interceptions as we passed abeam of Fances airspace.

When we were in sight of Cairo, we cancelled our IFR clearances and flew VFR to an Airbase in southern Egypt called ALPA One. We were housed in underground MIG hangers at the other end of the field where the AC-130s were parked. On 24 April 1981, the mission was kicked off. Every part of the mission was radio silent and by 1:30 A.M. the word was that the Delta Force had landed in Iran and was preparing to attack the Compound. At about 2:30 A.M. radio silence was broken and the raid was called off.

The General in charge of the operation at Alpha One ran into our compound stating "The mission just went to hell." He told me to get him a flight plan for a tanker to fly to the Indian Ocean, off load fuel and recover into the island of Diego Garcia. I woke the lead navigator and had him prepare the flight plan. When I told him what the general wanted done, his eyes became like a deer looking into a car's headlights and then he said, "we don't have the right maps for that area." The navigators failed to bring detailed maps of the Indian Ocean. Why we didn't have worldwide maps with us I will never know! I told him I used to do it all the time using high altitude enroute charts when flying into Hong Kong flying CINCPAC. It was not as accurate, but it got the job done.

I estimated the time and distance using High Altitude Enroute charts. I gave him an estimate and we launched one of our tankers. We figured they would have enough fuel to get to the Indian Ocean to refuel Navy fighters with about 20,000 pounds of fuel and still make it to Diego Garcia with 10,000 pounds of fuel reserve.

On the way past Lybia the tanker was jumped by a MIG 17. The tanker pilot dove the aircraft into the clouds and picked up just over super sonic speed which put them out of range of the MIG. They did get to the refueling area in time though no fighters were there. They waited 20 minutes and headed for Diego Garcia, The engines were overheated by the time they got there, due to the aircrew's efforts to avoid the MIG aircraft that jumped them, and they had to replace the engines.

About 6:30 the next morning, I woke up and looked out of our MIG hanger to see two camouflaged C-141s parked in front of the next hanger. I walked over to the hanger and walked through. There were over a hundred DELTA force individuals and the Marine helicopter pilots taking care of their wounds. A lot of them were bloodied up pretty bad. We were listening to the VHF radio and could hear the Iranians broadcasting that over 500 Americans had invaded the country and were attacking the Capital. The Delta force had landed and evacuated 4 hours earlier and the Iranians didn't know it at the time.

When we returned from the secret mission, we still had to keep it a secret and were awarded a Medal for Humanity Services award. The crew that flew to Diego Garcia was personally awarded the Flying Cross by the President.

After the Hostage Raid, our support of the Rapid Deployment Force continued supporting operations in Africa and South America. Though most of our missions were now becoming routine, I was ready for another change.

I contacted Colonel Honeywell and Bob Owen (a high ranking civilian) at Wright-Patterson AFB and told them I was ready to come back if they had an acquisition program which was in trouble and needed my expertise. They obviously relayed this request up the chain of command, because one day, while we were waiting for an Operational Readiness Inspection team to arrive unannounced, Major General Bill Thurman landed at Grissom AFB with no prior notification. He landed and was met by Colonel Wallace, the Wing Commander. The Colonel was expecting the Inspection team and asked the General if he needed anything and what his purpose of the visit was. The General told him he was stopping in to see Lieutenant Colonel Pumroy and would like to have lunch with him alone.

The Colonel found me at the alert shack and had the General with him. To my pleasure the Colonel was upset because he wasn't invited to come with us.

I met the General and we drove off-base to have lunch in private. He asked me if I was interested in coming to Wright-Patterson AFB to manage the procurement of support equipment, technical data and training equipment for the now revitalized B-1B program. I would have a budget of $2.5 Billion out of $22 Billion for the total program and would supervise over 20 people. He didn't have a manpower slot yet but could use me as soon as possible to get the program started. He asked me "how fast I could get there". I told him I could be there tomorrow if he could arrange it. Thirty days later I had an assignment to Wright-Patterson AFB as the Director of Logistics for the KC-10 program.

Before I left I did get one more thrill flying a RT-135 on a fly-by for Colonel Williams, the Vice Wing Commander who was retiring. I arranged to fly along on a mission with a Standardization Evaluation crew evaluating one of the crews under my supervision. When we returned to the base, I got into the pilot's seat to fly the fly-by. The aircraft was light as we had off loaded most of the fuel and only had about 12,000 pounds left. We orbited off the end of the runway until the ceremony started. When the Star Spangle Banner started playing one of our pilots let us know by UHF radio. Then all of a sudden he said the music was about to end. So I racked up about 80 degrees of bank and accelerated in a descent to arrive before the music stopped. When the airspeed got over 300 knots and altitude under 200 feet, I told the Instructor pilot to make sure I didn't exceed the airspeed limit and I would be looking out side to line the aircraft up and to avoid any birds. I don't know how fast or how low we got but they both exceeded the FAA rules of flight.

I lined up down the main street where the retirement ceremony was being held and when the crowd went under the nose of the aircraft I pulled up at about a 45 degree climb angle and disappeared through a thin layer of clouds at 10,000 feet. The attendees said it looked great with steamed air flowing off both wing tips and the sound of the engines as we accelerated out of site. The Colonel had tears flowing from his eyes and said it was the most moving thing in his life in the last 30 years.

No one complained about my violation of the flight rules, except during my going away party the Stan Eval pilot presented me with a "Pink Slip" for failing the check ride. Now we were off to Wright-Patterson AFB, Ohio.

CHAPTER TEN
Back to Wright-Patterson
Air Force Base

We arrived at Wright-Patterson AFB in July 1981. Before reporting in to personnel, I met with Lieutenant Colonel John Phillips who had just been promoted to full Colonel and was being transferred out of the KC-10 Program Office. I was to fill his position, and I wanted to talk to him before he left to see what I was getting into.

When arriving at Air Force Logistics Command (AFLC) headquarters to check in with personnel, I stopped by the General's office as I had heard General Mullins was now the Commander in Chief of AFLC. Ms. Jo Smith was his secretary and she knew me from my previous assignment. I asked her to let the General know I was in town and would like to see him sometime. About that time one of his executives came by with a paper for the General to sign. Jo told me to wait while she took the letter in to be signed and she would let the General know I was waiting. When she came out she said the General would see me.

I gave him a smart salute, he welcomed me back and asked where I was being assigned. I told him I was to replace John Phillips in the KC-10 Program, but that Major General Thurman wanted me to come work for him in the B-1B Program.

The General proceeded to review each of the programs with me and gave me the good and bad about each program. He asked me which I wanted to work on. It was a tough decision, as in the KC-10 job I would report directly to General Mullins (4 stars) and in the B-1B job I would report to Major General Thurman (2-stars). I asked him what he would do in my shoes. He said he would go where the action was and to see at what point the KC-10 would go organic depot support. If the KC-10 would have to go organic within a year or two that would be the best move.

I thanked him an went back to find out the KC-10 was only going to buy 80 airplanes and the break point was 120 airplanes. I gave him a call with the results and he said he would recommend going to the B-1B program as it needed more help. This didn't make the personnel guys too happy because this meant they would have to put in a request to the Military Personnel Center to change my assignment from under Air Force Logistics Command to Air Force Systems Command. Luckily my old home town buddy Chief Master Sergeant Vern Pfledderer was in rated assignment in the headquarters and he helped work the package. I stayed in the B-1B program until I retired in March 1985.

There were a lot of problems in the B-1B program as my area was under funded by over $500 Million and we had a cap on the spending which we couldn't exceed. To meet mission requirements, our B-1B management team had to procure support equipment using unique processes such as using existing equipment already designed for other weapon systems and by breaking out the procurement of many support equipment items to small businesses. Another process that saved millions of dollars was to centralize the development of depot software repair packages to save on hardware and manpower costs. Bottom line was that we found ways to make up for the $500 million shortfall and come in on budget.

My retirement came earlier than expected due to a particular feature of the promotion system which was changed but caused the promotion board to pass me over. This particular story starts when I was assigned to Grissom AFB, Indiana. I had just been promoted to Lieutenant Colonel and after changing jobs I was given an Officers Efficiency Report (OER) which included a closed form on the promote ability of the individual. All the Lieutenant Colonels who were promoted contributed money for a promotion party and I put the cost (approximately $400) on my club bill. Three months later I had another party for my relatives and friends which cost approximately $300 that I also put on my club bill. What I didn't know until later was that the Wing Commander was monitoring everyones club bill and he annotated a "potential drinking problem" on my closed evaluation form. This was enough to get me "passed over" even though I had received a "three star" endorsement each year I was at Wright-

Patterson which put me in the top 25 percent of the Lieutenant Colonels up for promotion.

Everyone, including me, was surprised when I was passed over for Colonel. I was initially mad at the Air Force for not recognizing my value as a senior officer, but then reality sat in and I accepted the fact that I was not going to be a general so it was time to change directions. I had a lot of support from friends at Wright-Patterson and the local industry, who provided leads for several program management jobs opportunities, some in the local area and some in other parts of the world. When I told General Thurman that I was retiring he tried to talk me into staying as he had been passed over for Colonel also. He even brought in General Skantz one weekend to talk me into staying in by guaranteeing me a "four star" endorsement and the number one position for the next board. Though I was extremely upset with the Air Force for not getting promoted, it was probably the best thing that could have happened to me. If I would have been promoted I would have been assigned to some remote location for a year and I had just found out our son Rick had a type of dyslexia in his eyes that had gone undetected for a several of years. He needed me around to keep him positively going in the right direction as I was afraid he was going to flunk out of school or drop out if he didn't have my support from home.

After retirement, I was also offered a consultant job with Dayton Aerospace Company who went into companies and reviewed there internal procedures in dealing with the Department of Defense. During this six month period they helped me establish a consulting company of my own. So now I had to refocus my career goals from climbing the military ranks to proving I could be successful in the civilian business world.

CHAPTER ELEVEN
Starting My Own Business

Several of my friends had started businesses to represent multiple businesses in obtaining government contracts. Joanne Hayden a small disadvantaged government representative told me I would make a good marketing rep representing multiple companies and should give it a try. The Small Business Office had names of companies who were looking for part time marketing people. I started a Sole Proprietary company named Acquisition, Logistics and Integration Consultants.

After contacting the companies on the small business office list, I signed contracts with 13 of them over a one-year period. This was too many for my brain to keep straight so I whittled the number of contracts down to six good companies. I also did what I call "technical consultant' services. For example: I hired a retired F-16 engineer and we did a study as a sub-contractor to VERAC corporation on the supportability of the F-16 Block 50 aircraft beginning in the year 2010. Later I did part of a study on all trainers in the Air Force inventory which VERAC won as a small business set-a-side out of the Air Force Logistics Command. That same year Ball Systems bought out the VERAC corporation so when it came time to re-bid the contract I had worked on they couldn't bid since they were now a large business. They asked me to find them a small business that would lead the effort and sub-contract 70 percent of the work to Ball Systems. After unsuccessfully finding a company I had an idea of how to do it. I asked my wife, Mary, if she would like to become a President of her own company (I couldn't do it as the AFR 30-30 stated that you could sell services but not hardware or software to the government if you were a commissioned Regular Officer – which I was). I was able to persuade her to take a chance by saying I would do the work – all she had to do was smile, meet and greet the people (I lied!).

We applied for a certification as an "S" Corporation under the name of Acquisition, Logistics and Integration Corporation and were granted certification on August 8, 1987. The proposal was due on September 1, 1987. With Ball Systems as our sub-contractor, we submitted the proposal on time and were notified on October 1, 1987 that we had won the contract.

We started work and in November 1987 the contract administrator was moved from Air Force Logistics Command to the Defense Contracting Auditing Agency. The Auditing Agency contacted us and informed us that we would need to have an audit of our financial procedures and books. I told him we should be exempt per the contract from having an audit since we were a start up small business. He informed me that was an AFLC policy and not theirs. They required an audit for all companies with first time contracts with the government. I told him we didn't have formal books yet since we hadn't received any payments from the government or billings from our sub-contractor yet. He asked me how we were doing the work and I told him we were doing it under the risk of not getting paid.

Our first meeting with the auditor didn't go too well since he didn't agree with most of my assumptions in the computation of our overhead and general and administrative costs. I told him we formed the company to help the government out since myself and Ball Systems had done all the preliminary work which was required to accomplish the next phase of the program. I said we wanted to do it the right way but needed some recommendations from him since I was an old country boy who had to milk cows while growing up. To my surprise he was an old country boy who milked cows before and after school also and he volunteered to come by the house after work and help me set up the books. "The Old Farm Boy" trick worked again. Needless to say we passed our first audit and were on our way to getting a "Facility Clearance" for Secret documents.

Mary was not too happy about this but that wasn't as bad as when I told her she would have to certify as a "Security Officer" for the corporation (she almost divorced me over this one).

I continued representing companies under the Sole Proprietary company for over nine years and continue to performed consultant

71

services to this day. In the interim we even sold 60 percent of the Corporation to Joe Coleman, a half blooded Cherokee Indian and half black. We submitted the request for Article 8(a) certification as a small disadvantaged company so we could receive some sole source contracts from the Air Force. The package sailed through the State and District Offices but when it got to the Small Business Agency (SBA) in Washington a secretary from there had contacted a secretary at Wright State University where Joe was teaching one class a week but had tenure which gave him incentive for running a business. The clerk at Wright State University looked Joe up in the computer and it had him down as a 40 hour per week employee. So even though we had a letter signed by the President of the University validating that Joe only taught two hours a week, the SBA terminated the request and told us to apply again in a year. By that time Joe got a full time job with the University as a Provost Marshall and couldn't qualify for an 8(a) certification, so we bought the company back from him giving me 60 percent of the company and Mary 40 percent.

We kept the company going by doing small studies directly to the Air Force and sub-contracting to bigger companies for consultant services. One such sub-contract was in support of the Global Hawk test and demonstration program. The Global Hawk is an Uninhabited Air Vehicle (UAV) which provides reconnaissance data to the Warfighter from

Figure 3: Global Hawk on a demonstration flight

altitudes over 65,000 feet and has an endurance capability of approximately 40 hours. I assisted the Global Hawk test manager in developing integrated schedules for the demonstration and evaluation missions which required coordination with the prime contractors to make sure they could deliver the required airframes and sensor systems on time, the test range organization, the Navy fleet, the owners of the required Satellites and the Joint Forces Command. Any error in the plan provided a potential for wasting millions of taxpayers dollars.

With several last minute adjustments we were able to successfully fly and participate in over 20 live combat exercises that simulated actual wartime scenarios. The Global Hawk program was such a success that when the war in Afghanistan started in 2001, the Global Hawk flew combat sorties and provided sensitive photos and imagery to the Central Command shortening the war by several months. The significance of this was the Global Hawk program was not out of its Engineering Manufacturing and Development (EMD) program yet.

The next contract was with Defense Research and Associates to fly our Bonanza as a target aircraft for one of their Research Projects. This was a requirement of the Global Hawk and Predator programs in that to fly Uninhabited Air Vehicles in National Airspace you have to have a see and avoid capability equal to a human pilot. Through several studies done by the Air Force Research Laboratory, it was determined that a pilot could see an F-16 aircraft flying head-on at less than two miles. Using test data it was determined that to provide an equivalent capability we had to develop a system to identify an object on a collision course at approximately four to five (4-5) miles for the worst case to enable the person in control of the UAV to identify the situation and have time to maneuver the air vehicle out of danger.

To test our solution for this requirement, we installed a video camera initially on a helicopter then on a twin engine test aircraft then flew various scenarios using our Bonanza as the target aircraft. We flew four scenarios: 1. a head-on pass with 250 feet separation; 2. a head-on pass with 15-20 degrees of offset. 3. a head-on pass with a 45 degree offset. 4. a scenario where the target aircraft would overtake the aircraft with the camera at a 45 degree side angle and cross one mile in front.

Several times on the head-on passes we didn't see each other at all but the camera performed without exception. The suspense during these missions kept the adrenaline flowing to the maximum. We flew twelve of these missions during 2002, two in 2003, four in 2004, and four in 2005 all without a mishap, but it was exciting.

The company continues to be lucrative, though we will never be multi millionaires. The best part of staying small is that the stress level is less than it is for those running large businesses. If you have employees, you have to keep them happy and deal with their personnel problems. You also have to maintain their workload and find new work to grow the company in order to afford the overhead required to operate the company. I like the way the company is going now. Keeping it small and simple has allowed Mary and I to have additional time to spend with our children and grandchildren, and to give back to the community.

CHAPTER TWELVE
Other Small Airplane Experiences

Though I had flown a small airplane when I was eight years old, I hadn't flown a single engine, propellar driven airplane since soloing in 1964. The next opportunity was in October 1965, after graduating from pilot training. I was now a "shit hot" Air Force pilot who could fly anything. So I took my dad to the South Bend airport in Indiana to rent an airplane. The owner of the airplane rental office was out flying a training mission and his son was running the office. I asked him to name the airplanes available and he said, "A Cherokee – can you fly it"

Of course, I said "Yes" and showed him my pilots license. He gave me the keys and checklist. I reviewed the starting procedures, emergency procedures, and landing data. Dad and I hopped in and after studying the cockpit figured out how to start it. We taxied to the end of the runway and had to hold since the father was on final approach for landing with his student. I pushed the top of the rudder peddles to stop the airplane but to my surprise, nothing happened. It took me a split second to realize that the brakes were activated by a lever and not the rudder peddles, like all other small airplanes. I pulled the lever just before entering the runway threshold.

"Are you sure you can fly this thing?" my dad asked me.

I said, "Sure!" I knew that this had to be the only thing different from other small airplanes. At least I hoped so.

We took off for my brother's farm and found some smoke to determine the direction of the wind. My brother had mowed a strip down the middle of his cow pasture, which was about one half mile long (approx. 2,600 feet). We landed easily and taxied up to the old farm house to take everyone for a ride.

My brother, Russell, my uncle Anton, and Uncle Louie were the first to want a ride. This put our gross weight to about 750 pounds, which was probably over the max weight for takeoff. I say probably because I am still not sure what the maximum weight is for the Cherokee. The wind favored taking off in the opposite direction, so now we had to takeoff toward a tree line that bordered the road at the end of the field.

On takeoff, it took a while to get takeoff speed and a fence was coming up too quickly to abort, so I rotated and leveled off about 10 feet off the ground to pick up enough airspeed to get over the trees, the stall warning horn started to blow, which meant I was almost at stall speed. I attempted to pull back on the yoke but knew if I did, we would stall and crash. So I just eased back on the yoke with the stall warning horn blasting in our ears. Luckily, we just cleared the trees but on the other side of the road were power lines that were about 100 feet high. My only option was to go under the power lines. Everybody thought I did this on purpose to give them a thrill. I never told them any different.

The next couple of flights were less dangerous, as I used 30 degrees of flaps and mixed women and children on-board to keep the weight down. This experience was too close for comport and was the last time I flew in and out of a pasture.

After returning to Wright-Patterson AFB in 1982, my military flying was finished. However, in 1986 I was notified of a problem my tenant was having on the farm I had purchased in 1979 at Santuck, Alabama. It took around 17 hours to drive by car and about three hours to fly by air. A friend of mine, Judy Westerhiede, owned a Cessna 172 airplane so I asked her if she would rent it to me. She told me she didn't let anyone else fly it but she was off work the rest of the week and would fly me down to Alabama. We had an uneventful flight to Alabama landing at a small airport just outside of Santuck.

However, on the way back we ran into a rain storm just outside of Knoxville, Tennessee and Judy had her hands full as we had light to moderate turbulence, it was night and we were in the clouds with down pouring rain. The sweat buds were rolling off her forehead as she fought the turbulent air. I finally convinced her I could give her some relief at the wheel and took over the controls. It was all I could handle which made her more comprehensive and every time I would get close to a mile off course she would get on me to correct. Though I do think she was happy I relieved her as it gave her time to settle down. We made it through the storm and landed in Louisville for fuel. The rest of the flight was uneventful though just being in the air again got my flying bug started again.

Next, I went to ground school to pass the instrument test and after passing the test signed up for flying lessons. After three lessons I passed the instrument in-flight exam and was cleared to fly solo in instrument conditions. After checking out I borrowed Judy's airplane to fly to Indiana to pickup my mother. I had only landed at Phillipsburg Airport one time and that was with Judy. So when I returned with my mother I could see the runway from about 10 miles out and thought I was lining up with the runway on a straight in approach. I made one of my typical smooth landings but when I looked at the other end of the runway I saw a person waving his arms up and down as if something was wrong. I hadn't realized it but I landed on the taxiway between the two rows of hangers. It used to be the primary runway but it was closed and supposedly had an "X" at the end of the runway indicating that it was closed. The problem was the red paint had worn off and I didn't see it.

It didn't bother me much but it embarrassed Judy as the airport manager thought it was her at first. Now it was time to buy my own airplane as I had the itch to fly again.

When I returned from this flight I found two private pilots (Bill Von Gunten and Gary Hayes) who were looking for a partner in their Cessna 172. So I joined their partnership and bought a third of a share in the Cessna 172. I only flew 25 hours the first year but loved every takeoff and landing which is where the challenges of flight are. As the saying goes flying is made up of hours of boredom and minutes of shear terror.

The only touchy flight I had in our Cessna 172 was on a flight from Atlanta, Georgia to Knoxville, Tennessee at night. I again ran into a rain storm over the Appalachian mountains enroute to Knoxville. The moderate to heavy turbulence almost turned the airplane over and unknown to me was enough to jar the oil cap loose. So when I landed at Knoxville the airplane had oil all over the bottom of it and I lost enough oil that it didn't register on the oil measurement stick. Though I didn't fly long enough in that condition to ruin the engine it gave me a scare so I called Dan Gigenova and stayed over night with he and his wife. It took a pitcher of beer and dinner to get settled down. The next day the weather was still bad but good enough to get back to Greene County Airport safely.

My partners and I flew this airplane for a couple of years then decided to purchase a faster and bigger one. We found one in Georgia. I flew to a Electronic Warfare National convention in Warner Robins, Georgia and dropped Bill Von Gunten off to pickup our newly purchased Bonanza. It was old (1956 "G" model) but in great condition. The Bonanza would cruise at about 150 knots true airspeed which meant we could fly to Myrtle Beach in three hours with no wind component.

The first of only two hairy flights I had in the Bonanza was during the fall of 2001. We had a group of ex military officers who had gathered at least once a year to catch up on each others new life experiences on Friday, play golf on Saturday morning, play poker all night on Saturday and return home on Sunday after another round of golf. When I called the weather service on Friday morning they

"Our 1956 Bonanza in front of hanger at Greene County Airport in 2001. The airplane is a G35 model made in 1956 and currently owned by myself and Bill Von Gunten"

were calling for some rough weather but the extreme weather was not due until the next morning. So I checked the weather again an hour before takeoff which I routinely do to make sure the weather don't surprise me. The weather had worsened but was still within my airplane tolerances. So, in bad judgment, I took off for Atlanta.

The visibility was clear, but when I got over the Appalachian mountains I ran into some severe clear air turbulence which was vertical in nature. In fact it was so severe I thought the wings were going to fall off. I climbed to a higher altitude but that didn't seem to smooth the air out. About 50 miles out of my landing destination I called for terminal weather to find out the winds for all the airports in the area were coming off the nose from 60 to 90 degrees at 18 gusty to 28 knots. Our airplane restriction is a maximum of 17 knots of crosswind. So the only condition I was legal was when the winds were steady and 60 degrees of the nose. I had enough fuel to return to Greene County Airport so I decided I would make one landing attempt to see if I could keep it on the runway and if that failed I would return to home base.

I had gust all the way down to about 75 feet above the runway where the ground effect started to smooth out the airflow. I continued down to the flair and still was able to keep the airplane lined up with the runway with full rudder applied. I went ahead and landed but when I put the nose down the steering mechanism took over and started to veer the airplane off the side of the runway. I gently applied the rudder to steer the airplane back to centerline took a couple of deep breaths and thanked God for looking after me again.

The other hair-raising experience I had in the Bonanza was during a test flight on the See and Avoid projet with Defense Research Associates in August 2005. I was to take off from Greene County Airport and proceed directly to the test area while the other test aircraft was to take off from Wright Brothers Airport to meet us at the target area. I had a passenger named Joe who was to operate the protable Global Positioning System (GPS) and computer during flight. We did the pre-flight checklist, started the engine, and taxied out to the runway for takeoff. During the pre-flight checklist. One item is to make sure the door is closed and locked. I checked to make sure the door was shut and Joe said the door was locked, but just after takeoff rotation, Joe said 'there is a lot of air coming in form around the door." I checked the door again, and it had cracked open. This is not a critical problem, as you can fly with the door unlocked, but it is uncomfortable for the passengers.

I decided to fly into a closed landing pattern and flew around the airport in preparation for another landing. This is something you never practice and it is the kind of unusual situation where you have to be able to adjust quickly or mistakes can happen. Unfortunately, my adjustment was faulty. The pattern went smoothly as I turned base and final approach, descending to the runway in a tight pattern for landing. There was a maintenance person walking along the runway, where temporarily distracted me, though I quickly refocused my attention on keeping the airplane lined up for a smooth landing so we could close the door and take off again. I came in over the threshold and flared the airplane while pulling the power off. Something felt strange but I couldn't determine what it was until a radio call came from out of nowhere stating "Gear up!! Gear up!! I looked down and it was my gear that was still up!

Within a fraction of a second, I pushed the power in to keep the airplane from touching the runway, as the propeller had to be only a few inches off the runway. As the airplane started to climb, I lowered the landing gear and made sure the down and locked lights were on. Then, I pulled back the power to come in for the final landing.

After coming to a stop and realizing that I had just come within inches of destroying our airplane and possibly killing myself as well as my passenger, I stopped the airplane in order to regain my composure-I still had to take off again to get to the test area before the other test airplane got there. I took a deep beath and called out on the radio in the blind. "Thank you, whoever took the initiative to say something on the radio. You just saved my ass! God was with both of us!"

We took off and flew for four hours and had a very successful flight. However, when I landed for the final flight of the day, I went into base operations to personally thank the person who made the call. It was Don Smith, the airport manager. I thanked him again for taking the initiative to make the call that saved us. He said it must have been my day, as he just happened to look out and couldn't believe his eyes that my gear was up. The other thing he said was that someone must have been looking out for me. Three minutes after the incident, he went to make another call on the radio only to find the battery had gone dead. If I had been three minutes later, I probably would have crashed. I don't know how many lives God has given me, but I definitely need all I can get.

CHAPTER THIRTEEN
Challenges of Being a City Councilman

We moved from base quarters to Fairborn in January 1985, just before I left the Air Force. All three children: Leanna, Julia and Richard graduated from Fairborn High School and married local mates. Thus Fairborn became our home town. After living there for 10 years I started getting involved in some of the organizations and committees supporting the city such as: Community Development and Grant Committee, Senior Center Board of Trustees, Rotary Club, Lions Club, and Abiding Christ Lutheran Church. This involvement put me in contact with the leaders of the community and access to the internal problems and issues within the city.

Community leaders were disgusted with the way the City Manager was dealing with the various problems and issues and wanted to replace him. The only way to do that was to have the City Council agree on a vote of no confidence in the City Manager and have him replaced. The current City Council tended to go with whatever the City Manager proposed and wouldn't vote him out. So these city leaders went out and found people who were unhappy with the way the city was being managed and asked them to run for council in the 1999 election. I was one of those they asked to run.

I wasn't really committed to running at first, but since these leaders helped raise money for my campaign and gave me political guidance on how to run a campaign I ended up deciding to go for it. Since I wasn't well known in the city I had to write newspaper articles on my background and views on city issues. I also made a tri-fold handout for when we went door to door shaking hands, asking for their vote and responding to questions and complaints about the city. Mary and I spend several weekends going door to door meeting people to let them know who I was. We also set out campaign signs for name recognition. Most of the "old boy" network who met at Reed's Donut Shop every morning to solve city, county and country problems, told me I couldn't win because nobody knew me.

To their surprise, I ended up with the most votes of all the six people who were running for City Council. The leaders were ecstatic as all three of the people they backed had won. Now was the hard part, identify the problem areas and determine why the City Manager was not solving them. It took about four month to find out that the City Manager had his own agenda and was running the city as a quiet dictator rather than a participative manager. The council had a vote of no confidence and the City Manager retired. We went through a long search to find a replacement and ended up hiring the deputy City Manager.

The first two years were pretty quiet, as everyone was waiting to see what the new regime would do. Several of the key Directors had quit and with the economy in a slump the new City Manager was not able to turn things around and some of the same problems remained such as repairing local streets.

During the third year, people started coming to the City Council meetings, which were viewed on the local TV channel, protesting the lack of initiative taken by the City Manager and Council. Now we were being pressured to replace the City Manager again with his deputy, a rising "Star" who was hired for business development. After many hours of deliberation, the council again decided to have a vote of no confidence and provided the City Manager with a poor annual performance evaluation.

It took another four months to get a consensus of how to handle the situation within the City Council. The situation was resolved and the deputy City Manager was now the City Manager who had the confidence of the city leaders. So, I completed the last term of my four-year term working with the new City Manager. I learned a lot about politics and city management over the four years. However, this will be the last time I run for a political position in the city as the $1800 per year payment received is not worth all the time spent, aggravation and criticism received. However, the new city manager convinced me to run for another term to provide continuity on the council. So I ran again for a two-year term unopposed and served through 2005.

After the election, I found out that one of the Greene County Commissioners had announced that he was retiring. He was the main commissioner that kept Wright Patterson AFB and Wright State University involved with the economic and social actions within Greene County. Since, I strongly believed that these organizations were critical to the well being of the county, I decided to run for his seat. What I didn't know was that there would be five other candidates , and two of them were prepared to spend over $50,000 just to win the primary election. I started late but thought I could win on my experience. The big mistake I made was to try to do too much of the campaign work myself. I developed brochures, requests for contributions, and invitations to fundraisers. I received over $6,000 in contributions, which was enough for one mailing of brochures and a down payment on five road side signs. By the last two weeks of the campaign, I had spent this plus $10,000 of my own money but still needed to do two more mailings and purchase advertisements in the local paper.

Mary, my daughter Julia, and I had walked the streets of each city in the county knocking on doors and attending any meeting we could get into. After assessing the situation, I decided not to spend any more money, as it wasn't worth going into debt by another $15,000 to win what was going to be a close race for a salary of $59,000 per year. Well, I ended up in third place, and the person who was second did spend $50,000 of his own money. I learned a lot from the experience and got to know some really interesting people. It was a success from that perspective, but it convinced me that I was not a good politician, and I will never run for a county level or higher position again.

In 2005, the city manager, mayor, and other city council members asked me to run for another four-year term. I agreed but decided not to spend any money on the campaign and would accept the consequences. Luckily, the other people who were running didn't turn in their petitions to allow them to be approved as candidates by the voter registration officials, so I ran unopposed. I was also selected by the council to the deputy mayor position which just backs up the mayor when he is unavailable. The next decision will be whether or not I run for mayor in 2007 when the current mayor. Tom Nagel, runs into term limits. It takes a lot of time to perform the mayor's function, so I would have to retire from all of my other jobs or positions. But I will run if there isn't a good candidate to take his place, as the city is going in the right direction, and I don't want it to return to mediocrity. In addition, it is a good way to continue to serve those in need, which I feel is my last calling.

Since my political positions have ended, I have been able to serve the citizens of Fairborn by serving as president of the Fairborn Lions Club increasing membership from 12 in 2012 to over 80 members in 2022. Have also served on the Greene County Community Foundation Board, Greene County Airport Authority Board, Fairborn Rotary Club, and over 10 committees. I am still being blessed with the love of family and friends I have met over the years, and God who continues to give me good health to continue my destiny to Serve Others!

CHAPTER FOURTEEN
Getting Ready for Retirement

I have discussed some of the highlights and most significant experiences of my life. Now it is time to slow down and try to reduce my desire to experience dangerous situations. It is time to enjoy the company of my wife and children and try to teach the grandchildren the basics of life. I am sure the exciting times are not finished though as Mary and I plan to travel to new places in the world we haven't been to yet. I have been in every state in the United States and every major country in the Pacific: Guam, Okinawa, Philippines, Korea, Japan, Loas, Thailand, Cambodia, Vietnam, Hong Kong, Singapore, Bali Beach, Jakarta, Australia, Johnson Island, Denmark, Norway, Sweden, Wake Island, and Diego Garcia. Still have a lot of countries to visit in Europe though I have been in England, Egypt, Israel, Greece, Turkey, Germany and Austria. Mary has been in about half the United States and about half the foreign countries I have been in. So between traveling around the world and stopping in to see friends throughout the United States I am sure we will experience many more exciting experiences to extend my destiny of living on the edge.

www.ingramcontent.com/pod-product-compliance
Lightning Source LLC
Chambersburg PA
CBHW051547120626
46551CB00013B/1411